Giraffe

Did You Know?

- Giraffes live in the savannas of central, eastern, and southern Africa.

- Giraffes are among the world's tallest mammals, with males standing up to 19 feet tall.

- Giraffes are known for their long necks and legs, and their distinctive spotted patterns.

- Giraffes eat the leaves of tall trees, such as the acacia.

CALIFORNIA
Science

Macmillan
McGraw-Hill

Program Authors

Dr. Jay K. Hackett
Professor Emeritus of Earth Sciences
University of Northern Colorado

Dr. Richard H. Moyer
Professor of Science Education and Natural
 Sciences
University of Michigan–Dearborn

Dr. JoAnne Vasquez
Elementary Science Education Consultant
NSTA Past President
Member, National Science Board
 and NASA Education Board

Mulugheta Teferi, M.A.
Principal, Gateway Middle School
St. Louis Public Schools
St. Louis, MO

Dinah Zike, M.Ed.
Dinah Might Adventures LP
San Antonio, TX

Kathryn LeRoy, M.S.
Executive Director
Division of Mathematics and Science Education
Miami-Dade County Public Schools, FL

Dr. Dorothy J.T. Terman
Science Curriculum Development Consultant
Former K–12 Science and Mathematics Coordinator
Irvine Unified School District, CA

Dr. Gerald F. Wheeler
Executive Director
National Science Teachers Association

Bank Street College of Education
New York, NY

Contributing Authors

Dr. Sally Ride
Sally Ride Science
San Diego, CA

Lucille Villegas Barrera, M.Ed.
Elementary Science Supervisor
Houston Independent School District
Houston, TX

Dr. Stephen F. Cunha
Professor of Geography
Humboldt State University
Arcata, CA

**American Museum
of Natural History**
New York, NY

Contributing Writer

Ellen C. Grace, M.S.
Consultant
Albuquerque, NM

 The American Museum of Natural History in New York City is one of the world's preeminent scientific, educational, and cultural institutions, with a global mission to explore and interpret human cultures and the natural world through scientific research, education, and exhibitions. Each year the Museum welcomes around four million visitors, including 500,000 schoolchildren in organized field trips. It provides professional development activities for thousands of teachers; hundreds of public programs that serve audiences ranging from preschoolers to seniors; and an array of learning and teaching resources for use in homes, schools, and community-based settings. Visit www.amnh. org for online resources.

learning through listening

Students with print disabilities may be eligible to obtain an accessible, audio version of the pupil edition of this textbook. Please call Recording for the Blind & Dyslexic at 1-800-221-4792 for complete information.

C

**Macmillan
McGraw-Hill**

Published by Macmillan/McGraw-Hill, of McGraw-Hill Education, a division of The McGraw-Hill Companies, Inc., Two Penn Plaza, New York, New York 10121.

Science Content Standards for California Public Schools reproduced by permission, California Department of Education, CDE Press, 1430 N Street, Suite 3207, Sacramento, CA 95814.

FOLDABLES is a trademark of The McGraw-Hill Companies, Inc.

Printed in the United States of America

ISBN 0-02-284376-0/2

3 4 5 6 7 8 9 (110/055) 11 10 09 08 07

iii

Scientific Method

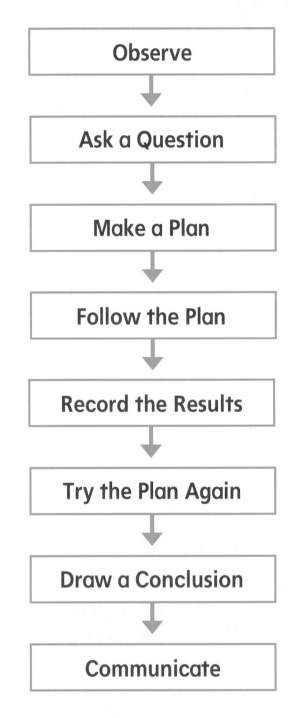

Observe

Ask a Question

Make a Plan

Follow the Plan

Record the Results

Try the Plan Again

Draw a Conclusion

Communicate

Be a Scientist

Life Science

▲ **An acorn can grow into an oak tree.**

▶ Amphibians live both on land and in water.

Earth Science

▼ **Strawberries grow well in California.**

Physical Science

▼ **A tug of war is a pulling contest.**

▶ **Air moving through a flute makes a sound.**

Activities

Life Science

▶ **Which seeds will
grow best?**

Earth Science

▲ **How would you sort these rocks?**

Activities

Physical Science

▶ **Which will fall faster?**

Reference

◄ **A hand lens shows a beetle clearly.**

Safety Tips

When you see ⚠ Be Careful, follow the safety rules.

Tell your teacher about accidents and spills right away.

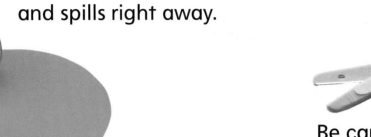

Be careful with sharp objects and glass.

Wear goggles when you are told to.

Wash your hands after each activity.

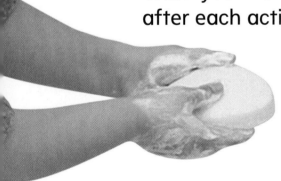

Keep your workplace neat. Clean up when you are done.

Be a Scientist

Sea anemones are animals
that look like plants.

What Is Science?

Have you ever wondered about things you see? If you have, then you are a scientist! Science is a way to understand the world around us.

4. Scientific progress is made by asking meaningful questions and conducting careful investigations. As a basis for understanding this concept and addressing the content in the other three strands, students should develop their own questions and perform investigations. Students will:

a. Make predictions based on observed patterns and not random guessing.

b. Measure length, weight, temperature, and liquid volume with appropriate tools and express those measurements in standard metric system units.

c. Compare and sort common objects according to two or more physical attributes (e.g., color, shape, texture, size, weight).

d. Write or draw descriptions of a sequence of steps, events, and observations.

e. Construct bar graphs to record data, using appropriately labeled axes.

f. Use magnifiers or microscopes to observe and draw descriptions of small objects or small features of objects.

g. Follow oral instructions for a scientific investigation.

Scientists use skills to answer questions about the world. Here are some skills they use.

observe

predict

communicate

measure

put things in order

compare

classify

record data

draw conclusions

Observe

Scientists **observe**.

Look at the picture. What do you see?

Predict

Predict means to use what you know to tell what will happen.

Scientists **predict**.

Look at the picture. What do you predict will happen when the weather gets warmer?

2 IE 4.a. Make predictions based on observed patterns and not random guessing.

Communicate

Inquiry Skill

Communicate means to write, draw, or tell your ideas to others.

Scientists **communicate** their ideas.

Share your predictions with others.

2 IE 4.d. Write or draw descriptions of a sequence of steps, events, and observations.

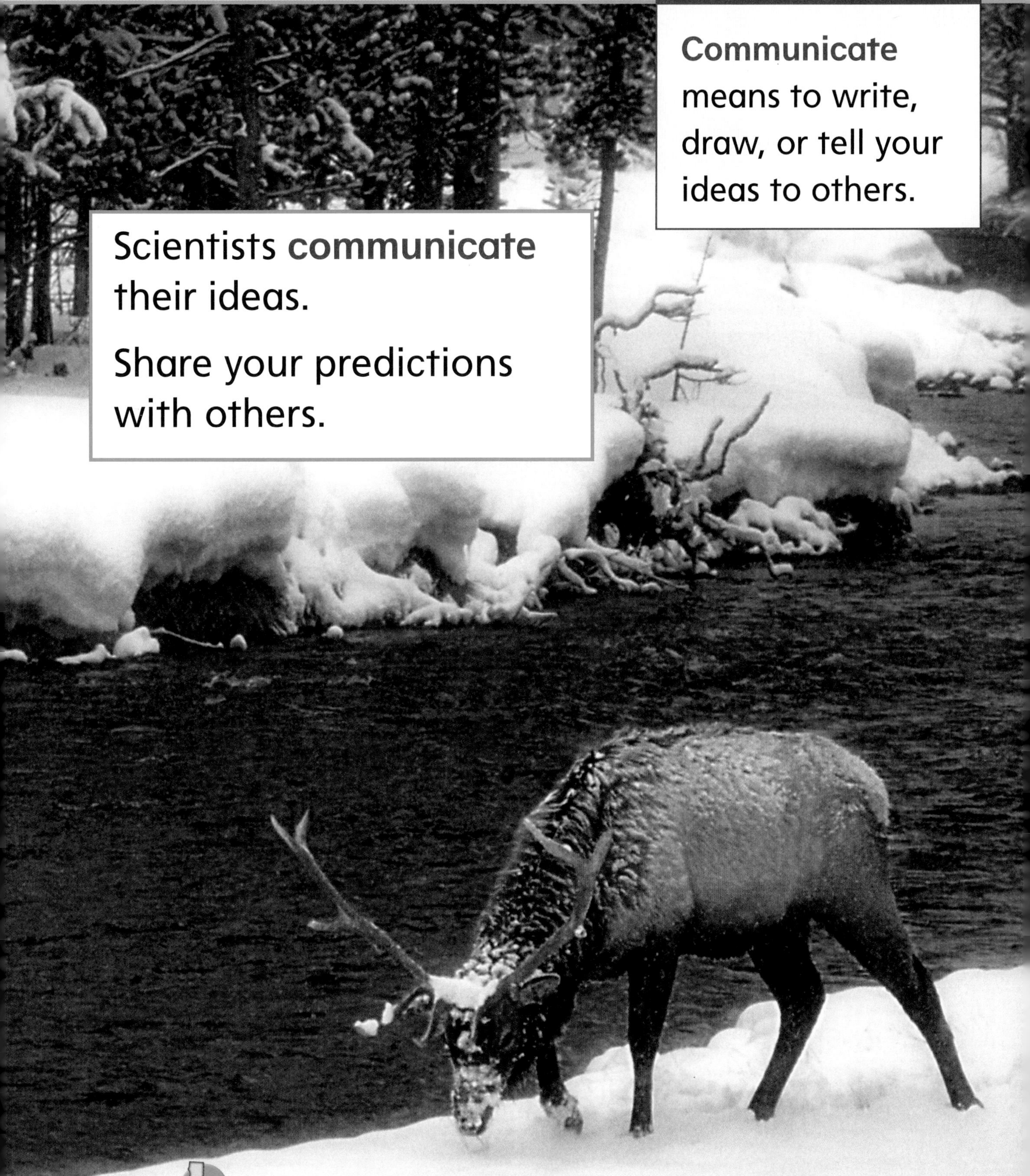

Measure

bird

Inquiry Skill

Measure means to find out how far something moves, or how long, how much, or how warm something is.

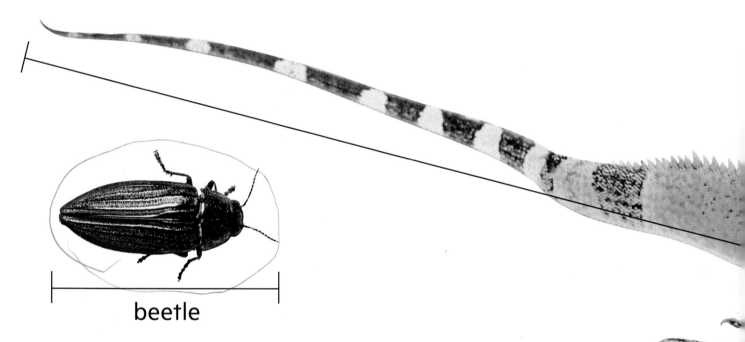

beetle

ant

Scientists **measure**.

Find out which animal is the smallest.
Which one is the largest?

2 IE 4.b. Measure length, weight, temperature, and liquid volume with appropriate tools and express those measurements in standard metric system units.

Sequence

Put things in order means to decide which comes first, next and last.

mouse

lizard

Scientists **put things in order**.

Put the animals in order from largest to smallest.

9

Compare

Compare means you see how things are alike and different.

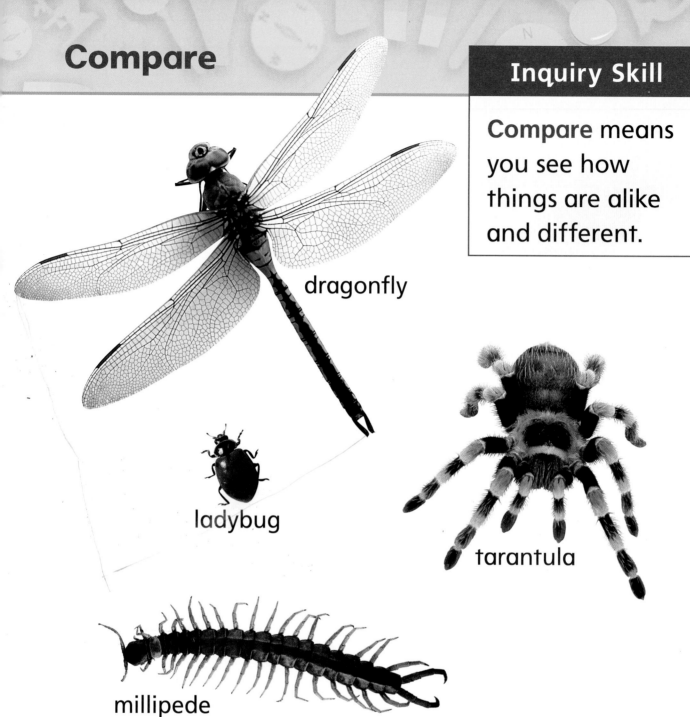

dragonfly

ladybug

tarantula

millipede

Scientists **compare** things.

Look at the pictures.
How are the animals alike?
How are they different?

beetle

 2 IE 4.c. Compare and sort common objects according to two or more physical attributes (e.g., color, shape, texture, size, weight).

Use Tools

Classify means to group things that are alike.

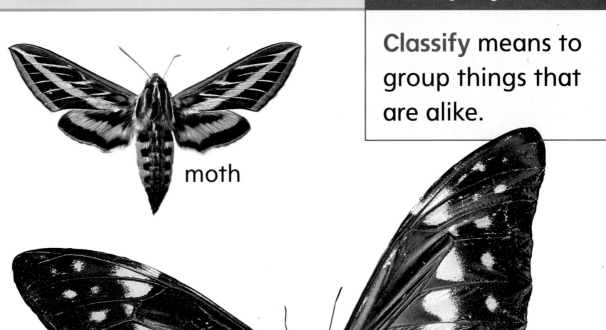

moth

butterfly

spider

Scientists **classify**.

Put the animals into groups that are alike.

Scientific Method

Scientists ask questions about the things they see. This plan helps them find answers to their questions. You can use it too.

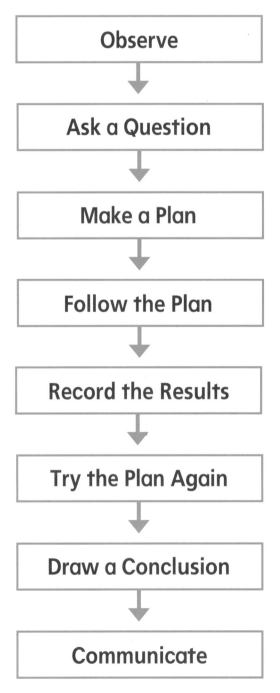

Observe

Ask a Question

Make a Plan

Follow the Plan

Record the Results

Try the Plan Again

Draw a Conclusion

Communicate

Observe and Ask a Question

Scientists **observe** and **ask questions**.

Is there something you want to know about animals? What do you think the answer to your question is?

Why do some animals blend in to their surroundings?

I think they blend in so that other animals cannot find them.

Make a Plan

Scientists **make a plan.**

How could you find the answer to your question? Make sure your plan tests only one thing.

Our Plan

1. Get black construction paper. Get red, white, and black dry beans.

2. Mix the beans together and put the beans on the paper.

3. Ask four people to pick up as many beans as they can in 10 seconds.

4. Record how many of each color bean they pick up.

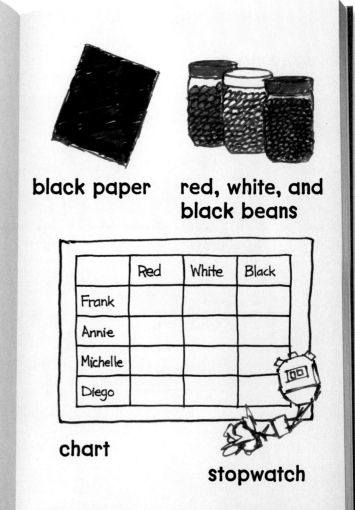

black paper

red, white, and black beans

	Red	White	Black
Frank			
Annie			
Michelle			
Diego			

chart

stopwatch

2 IE 4.g. Follow oral instructions for a scientific investigation.

Scientists **follow the plan.**

What will you need
to follow your plan?

Record the Results

Scientists **record the results.**

How will you record
what you observe?

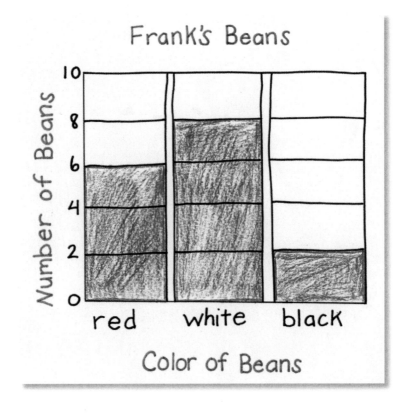

Number of Beans

	Red	White	Black
Frank	6	8	2
Annie	6	9	3
Michelle	7	7	3
Diego	7	8	3

Frank's Beans

Scientists **try the plan again.**

Were your results true?
Did you observe the same
thing each time you tried
your plan?

Draw a Conclusion and Communicate

Scientists **draw conclusions** and **communicate** their results.

Life Science

A turtle cannot crawl out of its shell.

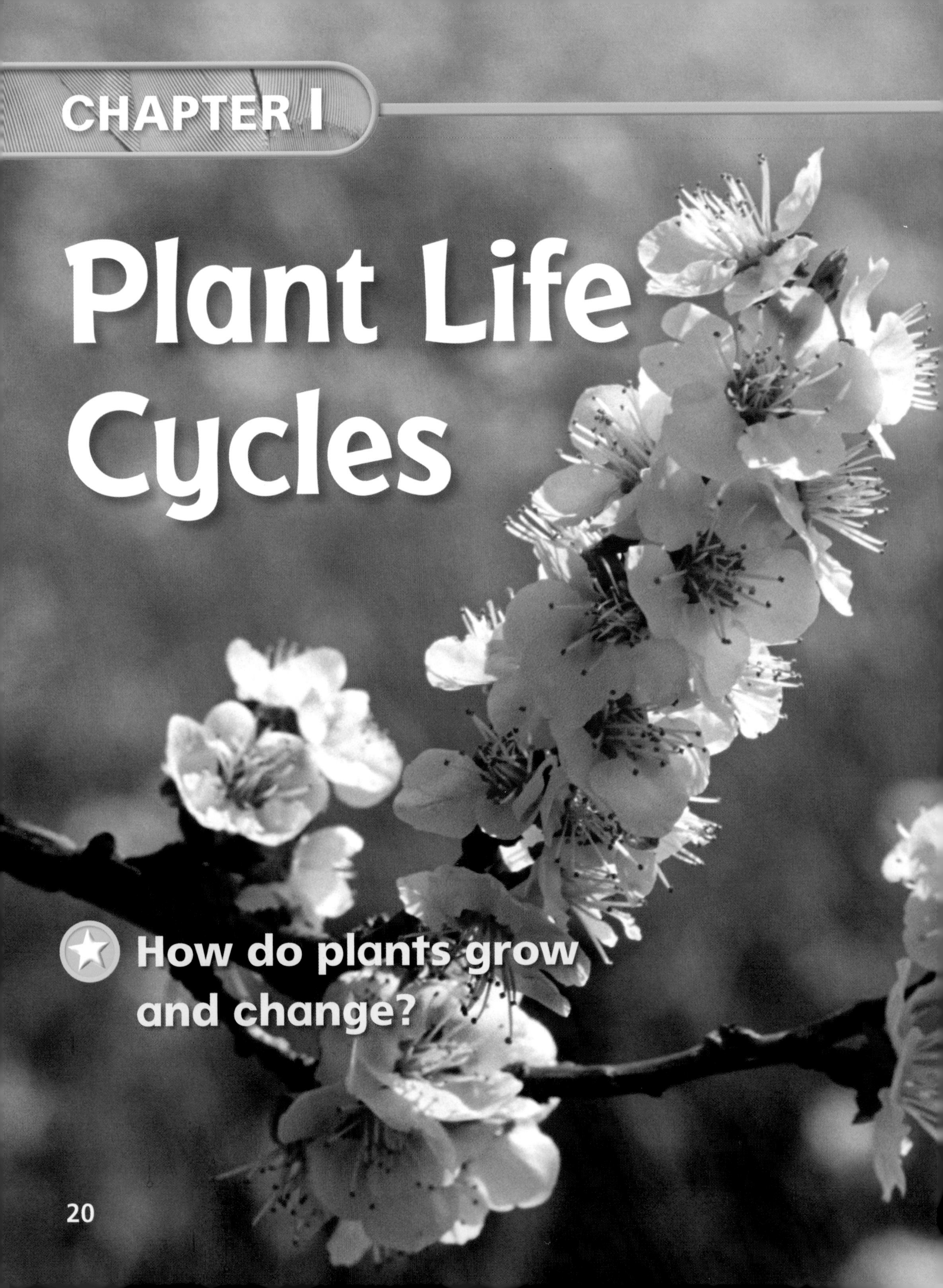

Plant Life Cycles

⭐ How do plants grow and change?

 2 LS 2. Plants and animals have predictable life cycles.

21

The Seed

by Aileen Fisher

How does it know,
this little seed,
if it is to grow
to a flower or weed,
if it is to be
a vine or shoot,
or grow to a tree
with a long deep root?
A seed is so small,
where do you suppose
it stores up all
of the things it knows?

Talk About It

What do you know about seeds?

Plants and Their Parts

Look and Wonder

Have you ever looked closely at a plant? What parts did you see?

 2 LS 2.f. Students know flowers and fruits are associated with reproduction in plants.

How are leaves alike and different?

What to Do

You need

hand lens

leaves

1. **Observe.** Use a hand lens to observe leaves.

2. **Communicate.** Draw pictures of what you see. What questions do you have?

3. **Compare.** How are the leaves alike and different?

Explore More

4. **Classify.** Sort the leaves into groups.

 2 IE 4.c. Compare and sort common objects according to two or more physical attributes (e.g., color, shape, texture, size, weight).

Vocabulary

flowers

fruit

seeds

What do roots, stems, and leaves do?

Most plants have roots, stems, and leaves. Plants use these parts to get light and water.

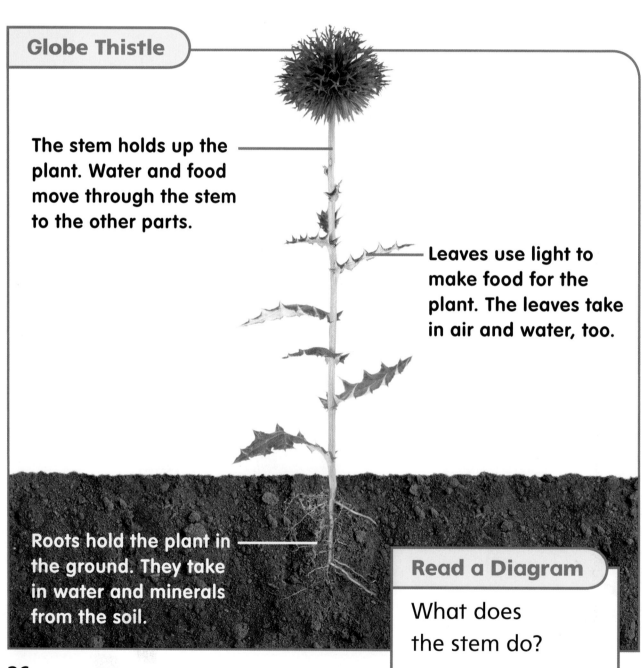

Globe Thistle

The stem holds up the plant. Water and food move through the stem to the other parts.

Leaves use light to make food for the plant. The leaves take in air and water, too.

Roots hold the plant in the ground. They take in water and minerals from the soil.

Read a Diagram

What does the stem do?

Plant parts look different in different environments. Plants that grow on the dark rain forest floor have large leaves. These help the plants take in as much light as they can. Desert plants have few or no leaves. These plants store water in thick stems. Some plants live in windy places. They grow long roots and short stems so they do not blow over.

 Why do you think desert plants have few or no leaves?

▲ **This Joshua tree grows in the desert.**

▲ **This banana tree grows in the rain forest.**

How can we describe roots?

Some roots are long and thin. Other roots are short and thick. Even though they look different, all roots help plants live in their environment. Some plants that live in dry places have very long roots. They grow down to find water deep underground. Some plants that live in wet places grow roots above the ground. This way the plant does not get too much water.

▶ **Globe amaranthus roots help the plant stay in the ground.**

▶ **This banyan tree lives in a wet place. Its roots grow above ground.**

Roots not only help plants, they also help animals. Bears, raccoons, and porcupines are just a few animals that eat roots. We eat roots such as radishes, carrots, and beets. What are other roots that we eat?

 What kind of roots might a desert plant have?

carrots

beets

What do flowers, fruit, and seeds do?

Many plants have **flowers**. Flowers come in different colors, shapes, and sizes. Even though they look different, all flowers make seeds. Inside a flower, there is a powder called pollen. Plants use pollen to make new plants.

▼ **A bee can move pollen from one flower to another.**

flower

▼ **We eat the flowers of the broccoli plant.**

Plants that have flowers also make **fruit**. Most of the time, a seed grows inside a fruit. The fruit keeps the seeds safe and helps them grow. We eat the fruits of many plants, such as peppers, apples, and blueberries. Some fruits like strawberries have seeds on the outside. A **seed** can grow into a new plant.

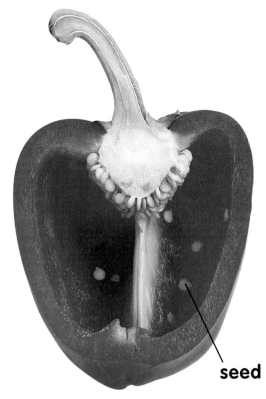

seed

pepper

 What other fruits do we eat?

Think, Talk, and Write

1. **Find the Main Idea.** What do roots, stems, and leaves do?

2. How does a fruit keep its seeds safe?

3. Write about some leaves you eat.

Health Link

How many leaves, roots, and fruits did you eat today? Make a list.

Observe

To **observe**, you use your senses to find out about something. You use senses to see, feel, hear, smell, and taste.

Learn It

You can use some of your senses to learn about flowers. You can write what you observe in a chart.

jasmine

jasmine

see	
feel	The leaves are smooth.
hear	
smell	The flowers smell good.

 2 IE 4.d. Write or draw descriptions of a sequence of steps, events, and observations.

Try It

Find a flower to observe or look at the pictures below.

1. What color is your flower? Which sense did you use to find out?

2. How do you think the leaves feel?

3. **Write About It.** Find another flower and compare.

Flowers and Fruits

Look and Wonder

How can this bean plant make new plants?

2 LS 2.f. Students know flowers and fruits are associated with reproduction in plants.

What are the parts of a seed?

What to Do

You need

dry lima bean

wet lima bean

hand lens

① **Observe.** Look at the dry lima bean. What does it feel like?

② **Observe.** Look at the wet lima bean. What do you see? What questions do you have about the seeds?

③ Use your fingernail to open the wet lima bean. Use a hand lens to look inside. Draw a picture of what you see.

④ **Communciate.** How did the water change the bean?

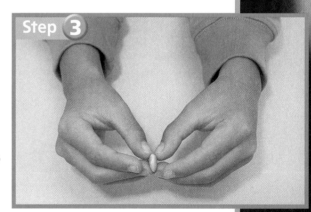

Step ③

Explore More

⑤ **Predict.** Do other kinds of beans look the same inside? Try it.

 2 IE 4.f. Use magnifiers or microscopes to observe and draw descriptions of small objects or small features of an object.

Vocabulary

stamen

pollen

pistil

seed coats

How do flowers make seeds?

Flowers have special parts so they can make new plants. The **stamen** of the flower makes **pollen**, a sticky powder. The **pistil** takes in the pollen and makes seeds. The seeds can grow into new plants.

Cantaloupe

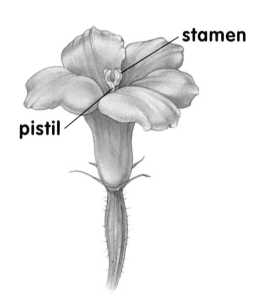

stamen

pistil

▲ Pollen moves from the stamen to the pistil. Then the flower starts to change.

▲ The flower grows bigger and the petals fall off. It grows into a fruit.

▲ The fruit protects the seeds inside.

Animals such as birds and bees can move pollen from a stamen to a pistil. Wind and water can move pollen, too. After pollen lands on a pistil, the flower starts to lose its petals. The flower begins to grow into fruit with seeds.

 Why do flowers need pollen?

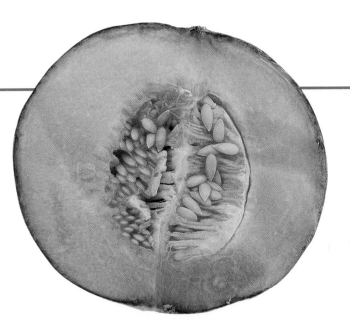

▲ The seeds inside the fruit can grow into new plants.

▲ After the fruit is ripe, it falls to the ground.

Read a Diagram

What happens after ripe fruit falls to the ground?

How do seeds look?

Most plants need seeds to make new plants. Seeds need light, water, and food to grow. Seeds have food inside them to help them grow. There are many different shapes and sizes of seeds.

▲ A marigold seed is small and thin.

star anise

◀ This pod is shaped like a star and it has many seeds. The shapes of the seed pod and the flower are alike.

Seeds have many parts. All seeds have **seed coats** which protect the seed. Seed coats also help keep the seeds from drying out. Some seeds also have hard shells.

 Why do you think some seeds have shells?

▲ Peanuts are seeds. They grow underground.

The shell is hard and light brown.

The seed coat of a peanut is thin and dark brown.

This part is a tiny plant. It will grow bigger and bigger.

This part gives food to the tiny plant so it can grow.

39
EXPLAIN

How do seeds move?

If seeds did not move, plants would always grow in the same spot. Animals help move seeds to new places. Many animals eat fruit and later they leave the seeds in the fruit behind. Some animals, like squirrels, bury seeds and may not return to get them. Some seeds stick to the fur of animals. The seeds get a ride to a new place.

◀ **This young baboon is eating a fruit with seeds.**

▲ **This bison is carrying seeds on its fur.**

Oceans and rivers can move seeds, too. Seeds fall into the water and they end up in new places. Wind can also move seeds. Some seeds are light enough for the wind to carry them far away.

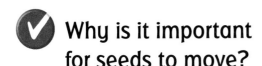 **Why is it important for seeds to move?**

▲ **The wind can carry this maple tree seed to a different place.**

Think, Talk, and Write

1. **Find the Main Idea.** What parts of a flower make new plants?

2. How would you take care of seeds to help them grow?

3. Explain how animals help plants make new plants.

Art Link

Draw pictures to show the seeds of different fruits.

Main Idea and Details

Read about a plant that uses wind to move its seeds The main idea is circled. The details are underlined.

Dandelions

Dandelions use the wind to move their seeds and make new plants. When a dandelion flower dies, its petals dry out. Then the seeds are ready to come off the flower. The seeds have long light tufts that help them float in the wind. The wind blows the seeds away to a new place.

 Write a Paragraph

Write a paragraph about a flower that you observed. Make sure you have a main idea and details.

Remember

The main idea tells what a paragraph is about. Details tell more about the main idea.

LOG ON -Journal Write about it online @ www.macmillanmh.com

 ELA R 2.2.5. Restate facts and details in the text to clarify and organize ideas.

How many seeds?

Some fruits, like watermelon, have many seeds. Other fruits, like peaches, have just one seed.

Solve a Problem

Suppose each apple on this tree had about 5 seeds. If you picked 3 apples, about how many seeds would you have? Show how you found the answer.

Write a number sentence about fruit seeds. Show your work.

Remember

You can draw pictures to help you find the answer.

MA NS 2.3.I. Use repeated addition, arrays, and counting by multiples to do multiplication.

Plants Grow and Change

Look and Wonder

Have you ever eaten an avocado? The seed is very big! How do you think the seed grows?

  2 LS 2.a. Students know that organisms reproduce offspring of their own kind and that the offspring resemble their parents and one another.

What will grow from a seed?

What to Do

1. Use toothpicks to hold your seed in a cup of water.

2. **Observe.** Watch how your plant grows. Remember to add water so that the bottom of the seed is always in water.

3. Draw pictures of your plant as it grows. What plant part grew first? What other parts did your seed grow?

Explore More

4. **Predict.** How will your plant change as it grows?

 2 IE 4.d. Write or draw descriptions of a sequence of steps, events, and observations.

You need

toothpicks

avocado seed

cup

Step 1

Vocabulary

traits

life cycle

SCIENCE QUEST Explore plant life with the Treasure Hunters.

How are plants like their parents?

You know that cats have kittens and dogs have puppies. Animals have babies that look and act like their parents. Plants work the same way. A sunflower makes seeds that grow into sunflowers. An oak tree makes acorns that grow into oak trees.

▼ **An acorn can grow into an oak tree.**

▲ **A sunflower seed can grow into a sunflower.**

The ways plants and animals look and act like their parents are called **traits**. Young plants will have many of the same traits as their parent plants. They will have the same shape of flowers, petals, and leaves. Some plants might look a little different from their parent plants.

 What are some traits of a sunflower?

▼ **These tulips look different, but they all need light, water, and food.**

What is a life cycle?

A **life cycle** shows how a living thing grows, changes, and makes new living things. The plant life cycle begins with a seed. It continues as plants make new plants.

Life Cycle of a Pine Tree

◀ **Adult pine trees make seeds inside cones.**

▲ **The cones fall to the ground. Some the seeds get moved to new places.**

◀ **A seed sprouts and becomes a seedling, or a young plant.**

▲ **The seedling grows bigger. It grows cones so it can make new plants.**

Read a Diagram

What does a pine tree make instead of flowers?

 LOG ON *Science in Motion* Watch a plant grow @ **www.macmillanmh.com**

All plants follow the same life cycles as their parent plants. Different plants have different life cycles. Some plants live for just a few weeks. Other plants live for many years.

▲ Redwood trees take more than two years to make cones.

✔ How does a life cycle start over?

◄ These flowers go through their whole life cycle in just a few months.

Think, Talk, and Write

1. **Find the Main Idea.** What are the steps in the life cycle of a plant?

2. How are a pine tree seedling and an adult pine tree alike? How are they different?

3. Describe the life cycle of a person.

Social Studies Link

Find out about fruits people in other countries like to eat.

Be a Scientist

You need

mixed wildflower seeds

egg carton

3 cups

soil

How are wildflowers alike and different?

What to do

1. **Classify.** Sort the seeds to find ones that look alike. Put the different types of seeds in an egg carton. Pick three different types. You will need two or three seeds of each type.

Step 1

2. Number the cups. Fill the cups with soil. Plant one type of seed in each cup.

Step 2

 2 IE 4.c. Compare and sort common objects according to two or more physical attributes.

3 Water the seeds. Put the seeds in a sunny place.

Step **3**

4 **Observe.** Watch your seeds as they grow. Record what you see every day. How long do they take to sprout? What shape are the leaves? How are the flowers alike and different?

Investigate More

Use the library or the Internet to find out the names of the plants you grew.

Plants and Their Environments

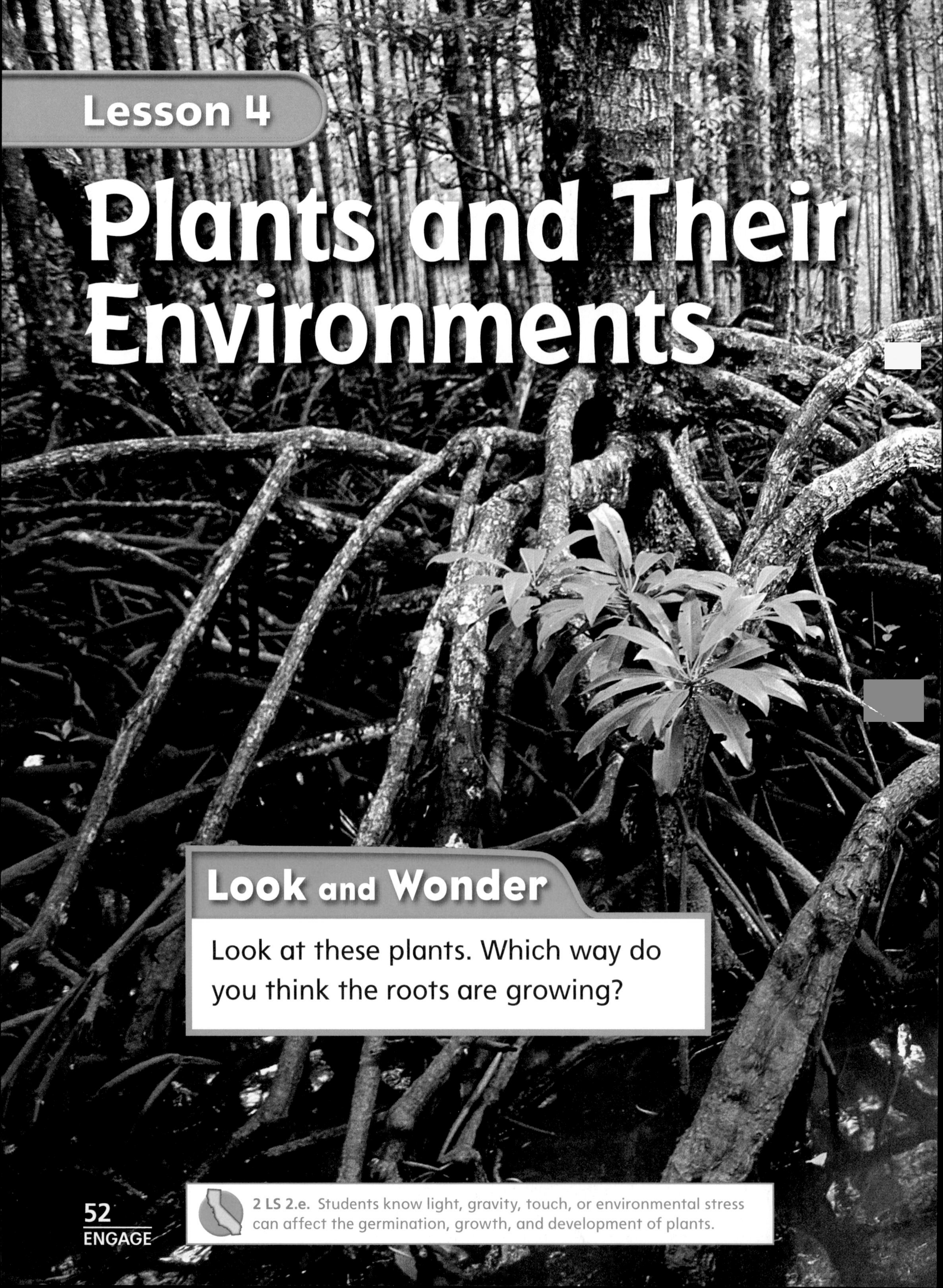

Look and Wonder

Look at these plants. Which way do you think the roots are growing?

2 LS 2.e. Students know light, gravity, touch, or environmental stress can affect the germination, growth, and development of plants.

How do roots grow?

What to Do

① Put a bean seed on a damp paper towel. Put it in the bag and tape it to a window.

② **Observe.** Watch the seed as it grows. Which part grows first? Which way do the roots grow?

③ After the roots have started to grow, turn the bag upside down. Tape it to the window again. Make sure the paper towel stays wet.

Step ③

Explore More

④ **Communicate.** Draw what happened to the roots.

 2 IE 4.d. Write or draw descriptions of a sequence of steps, events, and observations.

You need

bean seed

paper towel

plastic bag

tape

hand lens

How can plants change to get what they need?

You know that plants need light to grow. Plant parts can move to get more light. The stems and leaves of a plant can bend toward light. Flowers can turn toward light, too.

◀ **This plant bends toward the light that comes through the window.**

▲ **Some flowers will follow the Sun as it moves across the sky during the day.**

Some plants need soil to grow. They take in food and water from the soil. When a seed **germinates**, it begins to grow. The root always grows down. It grows toward the Earth to get what it needs. The stem grows up toward the light.

 Why do you think some plants have very large leaves?

lily pad

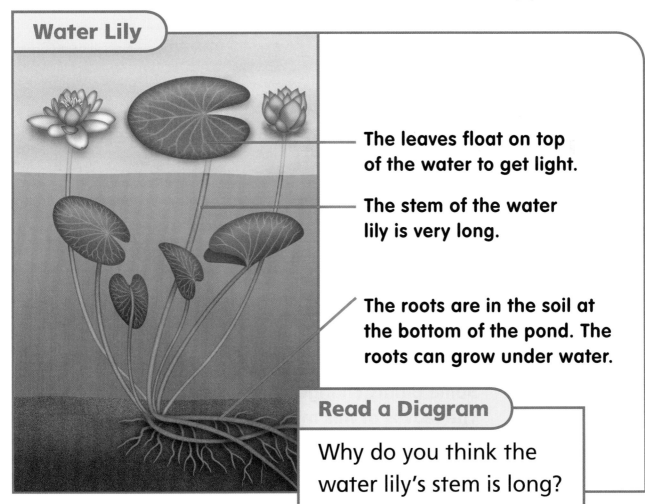

Water Lily

The leaves float on top of the water to get light.

The stem of the water lily is very long.

The roots are in the soil at the bottom of the pond. The roots can grow under water.

Read a Diagram

Why do you think the water lily's stem is long?

What traits help plants live in their environments?

Plants have ways to stay safe and get the light and water they need. Plants have traits that help them live in their environments. As a pumpkin grows, its vines will climb around things it touches. This helps the plant get light. Some plants, like the willow tree, have very long roots so they can get water deep below.

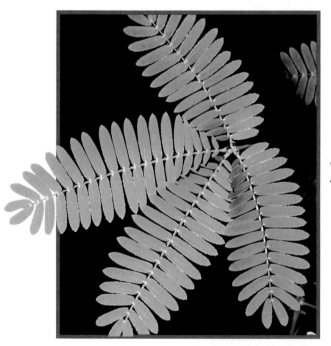 

Some plants change to stay safe. The leaves of this mimosa plant will fold up when they are touched. This way animals can not eat the leaves.

Some plants have changed to stay safe from the weather. On the coast, the wind is so strong that all the branches on the trees bend. They all grow in the same direction. The branches grow behind the trunk because it protects them from the wind.

 Why do you think some plants have thorns?

Think, Talk, and Write

1. **Find the Main Idea.** What changes the way plants grow?

2. Why might a plant have very long roots?

3. Write about what plants need to grow.

Music Link

Write a song about a plant that grows in a windy place.

The Power of Periwinkle

People who live in forests all over the world know about helpful plants. They use plants for food and to build homes. They also use plants to make medicine.

One helpful plant is the rosy periwinkle. It first grew in Madagascar, and later people spread it around the world. People now use the plant to treat fevers, sore throats, toothaches, and upset stomachs.

Today, some forests in Madagascar are being cut down. People clear the land to grow food. Scientists want to keep some of these forests safe. There may be more helpful plants to study and use.

Madagascar

ELA R 2.2.6. Recognize cause-and-effect relationships in a text.

▲ Scientists and local people use the rosy periwinkle to treat diseases.

Talk About It

Predict. What might happen to helpful plants if the forests were cut down?

 **e-Journal** Write about it online @ **www.macmillanmh.com**

AMERICAN MUSEUM of NATURAL HISTORY

59
EXTEND

Amazing Plants

This plant may look pretty, but it is dangerous! Poison ivy can grow on trees or spread out on the ground. The leaves can be small or as big as your hand! If you touch the plant you can get a rash. You should wash your hands quickly in cold water.

   Did you know that some plants
trap animals? The Venus flytrap
makes its own food, but also
catches insects. First an insect
lands on the edge of the trap.
Then the trap snaps shut on the
insect. The plant breaks down the
insect's body just as your stomach
breaks down food.

This is seaweed. Like all
seaweed, it grows in the ocean.
To get sunlight, this seaweed
floats on the top of the water. This
seaweed has little pods filled with
air. They help the seaweed float.
This seaweed is sometimes called
pop-weed. Can you guess why?

Cattails live in wet places. They can grow over ten feet tall! Fish, frogs, and geese hide among the cattails. The flower of a cattail is long and brown. When the flower dries up, the brown part splits open. Fluffy seeds come out and wind carries them away.

This chickweed lives in cold and windy places in Alaska. Its leaves have tiny hairs that help it stay warm. The plant grows on rocky hills. Its roots are short because they can grow down into the hard ground. To stay safe from strong winds, the plant does not grow very tall.

The prickly pear cactus lives in the hot, dry desert. Its roots do not grow deep. Instead, the roots spread out just below the ground. When it rains, the roots can soak up the water like a sponge. The needles on the stem and fruit help the cactus stay safe from animals.

Vocabulary

life cycle, page 48	**seed coat**, page 39
pistil, page 36	**stamen**, page 36
seed, page 31	**traits**, page 47

Use each word once for items 1–6.

1. The _____ of the flower makes pollen. 2 LS 2.f

2. The _____ takes in pollen to make seeds. 2 LS 2.f

3. A _____ of a plant shows how it grows, lives, and dies. 2 LS 2.f

4. Peanut seeds have a thin brown cover. This is called a _____. 2 LS 2.f

5   The ways plants and animals look and act like their parents are called _____. 2 LS 2.a

6. The _____ can grow into a new plant. 2 LS 2.f

7. Observe. Look at the pictures below. What traits do these plants share? 2 LS 2.d

8. Describe what seeds and seedlings need to grow. 2 LS 2.f

9. Discuss how you think desert plants live in their environment. 2 LS 2.e

 How do plants grow and change? 2 LS 2.e

CHAPTER I

How do plants make new plants?

Look at the pictures below. They are not in order.

▶ Draw the pictures to show the life cycle of a peach.

▶ Describe the life cycle of this plant.

2 LS 2.f. Students know flowers and fruits are associated with reproduction in plants.

1 **Which part of the plant grows into a fruit?** 2 LS 2.f

A leaf

B flower

C root

D seed

2 **Look at the picture below.**

What is happening in the picture? 2 LS 2.e

A A plant grows toward the light.

B A plant makes new plants.

C Seeds move to a new place.

D A flower uses pollen to make seeds.

3 **What do you do when you observe something?** 2 LS 4.d

A You tell what will happen next.

B You make a plan and try it out.

C You use your senses to learn about something.

D You tell how something grows, lives, and dies.

CHAPTER 2

Animal Life Cycles

⭐ **How do animals grow and change?**

 2 LS 2. Plants and animals have predictable life cycles.

In Payment

by Aileen Fisher

A caterpillar nibbles,
nibbles at a plant
until the leaves look ragged
and even rather scant.

And then the caterpillar
weaves a silk cocoon,
and turns into a butterfly
one sunny day in June,

And then he carries pollen
to blossoms red and pink,
which sort of pays for nibbles
that he nibbled, don't you think?

Talk About It

Where have you seen
a caterpillar?

Kinds of Animals

Look and Wonder

The world is full of animals! How many different kinds of animals can you think of?

2 LS 2.b. Students know the sequential stages of life cycles are different for different animals, such as butterflies, frogs, and mice.

How can we put animals into groups?

What to Do

① **Classify.** Make a list of ten animals. Put your animals into groups. What groups did you use?

② **Talk** about your animal groups with a partner. What groups did your partner use?

③ **Compare.** How are your groups and your partner's groups alike? How are they different?

Explore More

④ **Infer.** Why do you think scientists put animals into groups?

sea turtle

seagull

dolphin

sea otter

lobster

 2 IE 4.c. Compare and sort common objects according to two or more physical attributes (e.g., color, shape, texture, size, weight).

Vocabulary

amphibians

mammals

reptiles

How do we classify animals?

Scientists classify animals into several groups. Some animals have backbones and some do not. Scientists classify animals because there are so many of them.

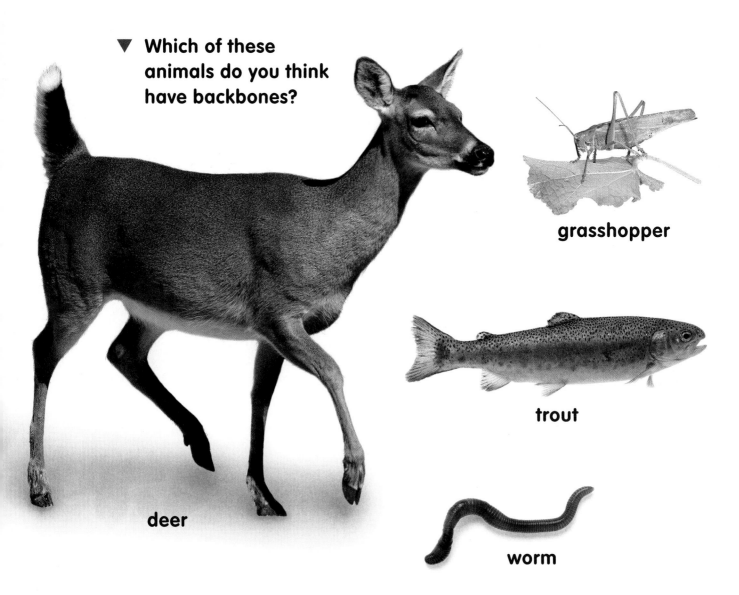

▼ Which of these animals do you think have backbones?

deer

grasshopper

trout

worm

hawk

Touch the back of your neck. Do you feel bumps? These are part of your backbone. Your backbone goes from your hips all the way up to your head. Not all animals have a backbone.

 What are other animals with backbones?

Squirrel Backbone

Read a Diagram

Where does the squirrel's backbone begin and end?

How can we classify animals with backbones?

Scientists classify animals with backbones into more groups. This helps scientists study and understand animals.

▶ Almost all **amphibians** begin their lives in water. They often have smooth, moist skin. This helps them live on both land and water.

salamander

▼ **Mammals** have hair or fur. They give birth to live young. Mammals feed their young milk.

lions

▼ **Reptiles** have scales and are cold-blooded. They need sunlight to stay warm. Most reptiles lay eggs.

alligator

◀ **Birds are the only animals with feathers. They have two wings and two legs. Not all birds can fly.**

bluebird

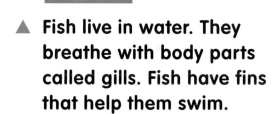

salmon

▲ **Fish live in water. They breathe with body parts called gills. Fish have fins that help them swim.**

✓ **What are other animals that could fit in these groups?**

How can we classify animals without backbones?

There are many kinds of animals that have no backbones. There are more animals without backbones than animals with backbones! Some animals without backbones have shells or hard body coverings. This helps them stay safe.

▲ The dragonfly has a hard body covering. It uses its wings to fly away from predators.

▲ The lobster has a hard body covering to stay safe. It uses its claws to break open food.

◀ The beetle has a hard outer shell. It has three body segments and six legs.

Some animals without backbones have no shells. They have soft bodies. These animals must use other ways to stay safe.

 What kind of body covering does a snail have?

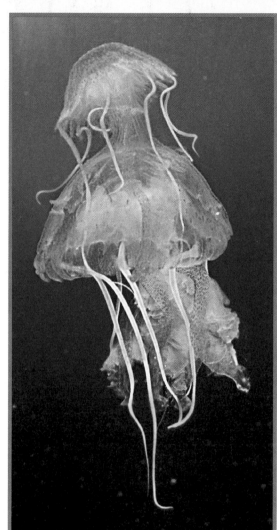

▶ These jellyfish have no hard body coverings. They sting other animals to stay safe and get food.

Think, Talk, and Write

1. **Classify.** Think of five animals with backbones and five without backbones.

2. How do you think a bee stays safe?

3. Write about an animal. What does the animal look like? How does it stay safe?

Music Link

Write a song about a beetle's shell.

Focus on Skills

Communicate

To **communicate**, you share your ideas with others.

Learn It

You can use a chart to communicate what you learned.

Different Animals		
Mammals	Reptiles	Birds
horse	lizard	eagle
mouse	turtle	sparrow

penguin

iguana

lamb

 2 IE 4.c. Compare and sort common objects according to two or more physical attributes (e.g., color, shape, texture, size, weight).

Try It

Use a chart to classify these animals. Add other animals to your chart. Share your chart with a partner.

parrot

guinea pig

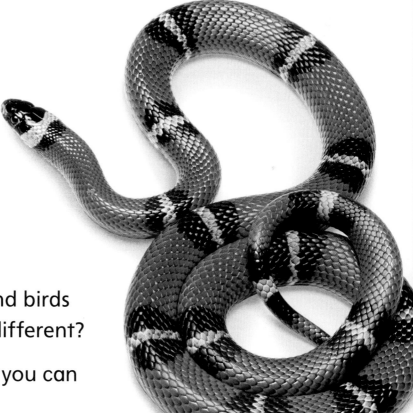
snake

1. How are mammals and birds alike? How are they different?

2. What are some ways you can classify the animals?

3. **Write About It.** How is your chart different from your partner's?

Mammals

Look and Wonder

How do you think these young mammals will act when they grow up?

2 LS 2.a. Students know that organisms reproduce offspring of their own kind and that the offspring resemble their parents and one another.

How are babies and adults alike and different?

What to Do

1. What do babies look like? How do they act?

2. What do adults look like? How do they act?

3. **Compare.** Make a Venn diagram to compare babies with adults.

Step 3

Explore More

4. **Compare.** How are a baby human and a baby rabbit alike and different?

 2 IE 4.c. Compare and sort common objects according to two or more physical attributes (e.g., color, shape, texture, size, weight).

How does a mammal grow and change?

All animals go through a life cycle, just like plants. Different kinds of animals have different life cycles. When mammals are born, they need their mothers to live. The babies get milk from their mothers. Then the babies grow and change into adults.

▼ **This baby panda gets milk from its mother. The mother keeps her cub safe.**

When a baby panda is first born, it needs a lot of help from its mother. The mother feeds and hides the newborn.

As the baby panda grows older, it begins to climb and play. The cub still needs its mother to find food and stay safe.

A young adult panda can find food on its own. It can have its own babies and the life cycle begins again.

Read a Diagram

When can a panda find its own food?

 How are a baby panda and an adult panda alike? How are they different?

How are baby mammals and their parents alike and different?

Young animals can look and act like their parents. Sea lion pups have a tail, flippers, and fur just like their parents. The pups also swim and eat fish just like their parents. All sea lions live in big groups and bark to communicate with each other. A mother sea lion and her pup share a special bark. This bark helps the mother and the pup find each other in the group.

California sea lions

Baby mammals can look different from their parents. A cat gives birth to many kittens. The kittens can have different color eyes and fur from their parents. Sometimes the kittens look different from each other, too. The kittens can be different sizes and colors. Even though the kittens look different, they all have four legs, a tail, and fur.

✓ How are these kittens alike? How are they different?

Think, Talk, and Write

1. **Classify.** Think of five animals that are mammals and five that are not.

2. How might a tiger take care of her cubs?

3. Describe the life cycle of a dog. Write about how the dog looks and acts as it grows.

Health *Link

What do people need in order to grow strong and healthy?

Meet Nancy Simmons

◀ Nancy Simmons is holding a false vampire bat. It is one of the largest bats in the world.

Nancy Simmons is a scientist at the American Museum of Natural History. She studies bats all around the world. She has found more than 80 different kinds of bats in one forest. Nancy learns about what bats eat and where they live.

▲ Bats are the only mammals that can fly.

ELA R 2.2.4. Ask clarifying questions about essential textual elements of exposition (e.g., *why, what if, how*).

Bats give birth to one baby at a time. The baby is called a pup. The pup is small and pink and it has no hair. To stay safe, the pup hangs on to its mother. The pup gets milk from its mother and grows bigger. After a few months, the pup is ready to fly. Soon the young bat leaves its mother. It can find its own food and start its own family.

▲ **Bats hang upside down.**

Talk About It

Find the Main Idea. How do bats grow and change?

 **e-Journal** Write about it online @ **www.macmillanmh.com**

Animals from Eggs

Look and Wonder

Why do you think some animals make nests?

 2 LS 2.a. Students know that organisms reproduce offspring from their own kind and that the offspring resemble their parents and one another.

How do birds keep their eggs safe?

What to Do

1 **Communicate.** Discuss with a partner what eggs need to stay safe.

2 Build a nest for an egg.

3 How did you make things stay in place without using tape?

twigs

chenille sticks

Explore More

4 **Communicate.** Look at pictures of real nests. What do animals use to keep their eggs safe?

string

 2 IE 4.a. Make predictions based on observed patterns and not random guessing.

Step 2

Vocabulary

larva

molting

pupa

SCIENCE QUEST Explore animal life cycles with the Treasure Hunters.

Why do many animals lay eggs?

Birds are not the only animals that lay eggs. Reptiles, amphibians, and fish all lay eggs. Insects and many kinds of sea animals lay eggs, too. A queen bee can lay more than 2,000 eggs in just one day! Animals lay many eggs because some of their babies will not survive. Many young animals might get eaten by other animals.

◀ **The queen bee lays thousands of eggs in combs.**

▼ **Salmon also lay thousands of eggs. They lay their eggs in between rocks in rivers.**

▼ **This sea turtle is burying its eggs in a sandy nest to keep them safe.**

Many animals that lay eggs do not take care of their young. Female sea turtles come on to the shore and dig holes. Then they bury their eggs in the sand and leave. A female sea turtle can lay up to 150 eggs! When the eggs hatch, the young must find their own way to the ocean. They must learn how to live on their own. Many young turtles get eaten by other animals like seagulls.

 How does an egg protect the animal inside?

▲ **Baby turtles must find their own way to the sea. Sometimes people help by keeping away other animals who want to eat the turtles.**

How do animals from eggs become adults?

Most eggs have an outside shell or covering that keeps the growing animal inside safe. The egg also keeps the young animal from drying out. After the animal is fully formed, it hatches from the egg.

Crab Life Cycle

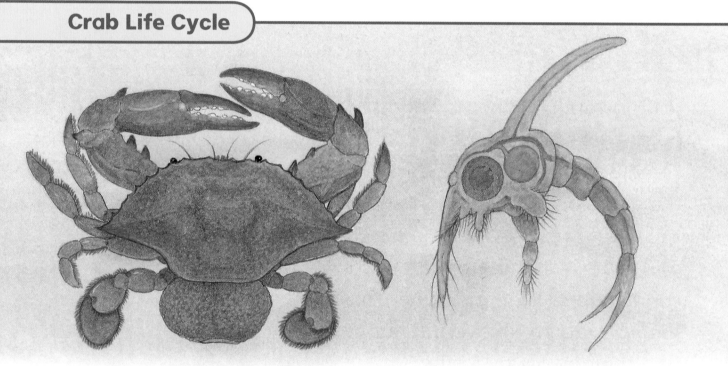

▲ The adult female crab lays many eggs in a spongy clump that sticks to her body.

▲ After 2 weeks, the eggs hatch. A crab larva comes out of the egg. The larva looks very different from its parents. The larva begins to eat and grow.

The animal grows bigger and becomes an adult. Then it can have its own young and the life cycle begins again.

 What animals lay eggs that do not have shells?

▲ After 5 weeks, the young crabs must shed their shells so they can grow bigger. This is called **molting**.

▲ The crab keeps growing and molting. After about 16 months, the crab becomes an adult. It is ready to lay eggs of its own.

Read a Diagram

Why do crabs molt?

 *Science in Motion* Watch animals grow @ **www.macmillanmh.com**

How does a butterfly grow and change?

Butterflies begin life looking very different from their parents. They go through four stages as they grow into adults.

 Why do you think some butterflies lay each egg on a different leaf?

▲ Butterflies lay their eggs on leaves or branches. Some butterflies lay many eggs in one spot. Others lay each egg in a different spot.

▲ After ten days, the egg hatches and a caterpillar comes out. The caterpillar is a larva. The larva eats leaves and grows.

Think, Talk, and Write

1. **Classify.** Think of five animals that lay eggs. What groups do they belong to?

2. How are the life cycles of crabs and butterflies alike and different?

3. Write about the life cycle of a bird.

Social Studies Link

Find out about some butterfly folk tales from other cultures.

LOG ON e-Review Summaries and quizzes online @ www.macmillanmh.com

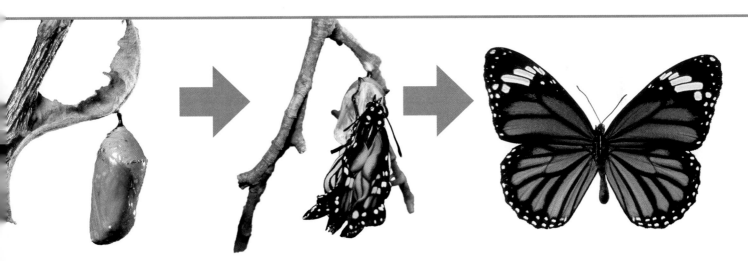

▲ After three weeks, the caterpillar spins a thread around itself, making a hard case. Now it is a pupa. Inside the hard case the pupa changes into a butterfly.

▲ When the butterfly is fully grown, it crawls out of the hard case.

▲ Now the butterfly is ready to fly, eat nectar from flowers, and lay eggs of its own.

Be a Scientist

You need

oatmeal

container

hand lens

mealworm larva

slice of apple

ruler

How does a mealworm grow?

Find out how a mealworm grows and changes.

What to Do

1. Put some oatmeal in the container. Poke holes in the lid.

Step 1

2. **Observe.** What does a mealworm look like? Place a mealworm and the apple slice in the container.

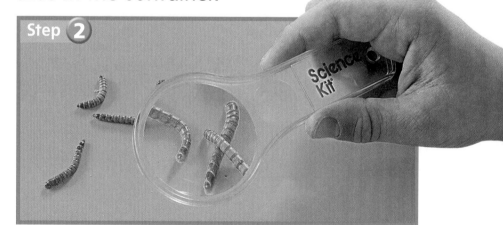

Step 2

 2 IE 4.d. Write or draw descriptions of a sequence of steps, events, and observations.

3 **Record Data.** Measure your mealworm every two days. Remember to be gentle with the mealworm. Write about how the animal changed.

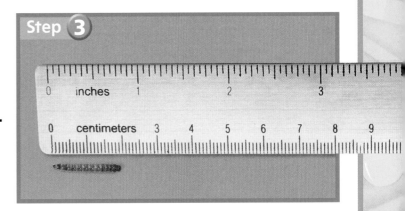

Step **3**

4 **Predict.** How long do you think your mealworm will grow? How do you think it will change?

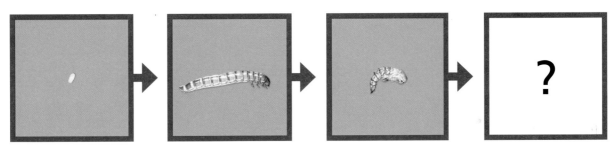

?

Investigate More

Compare. Observe another mealworm. How are they alike and different?

Animal Traits

Look and Wonder

Why do you think these zebras have different stripe patterns?

 2 LS 2.d. Students know there is variation among individuals of one kind within a population.

How are these zebras alike and different?

What to Do

1. Observe these zebras.

2. **Compare.** How are they alike and different?

3. How do you think stripes help zebras stay safe?

Explore More

4. **Compare.** Find pictures of another animal with a pattern. Observe how the patterns are alike and different.

2 IE 4.c. Compare and sort objects according to two or more physical attributes (e.g., color, shape, texture, size, weight).

Vocabulary

population

How do traits help animals?

You learned that the ways plants and animals look and act like their parents are called traits. All animals have special traits that help them live in their environments. These traits can be their color, their body parts, or a way they act.

▲ Male peacocks have bright feathers and sing loud songs so females can find them.

▶ Giraffes have long necks so they can eat leaves that are high in the trees.

Animals use their traits to stay safe. Some animals can fly away when they are in danger. Other animals can blend into their environments. Another way animals stay safe is by fighting off other animals. The bites of some snakes and spiders can be poisonous.

 What traits help a bird to stay safe?

▲ **One of the most dangerous animals in the world is the poison dart frog. It lives in South America.**

Tortoise

Read a Photo

How can this tortoise stay safe?

What is a population?

A **population** is a group of the same kind of animal that lives near each other. For example, the black bears that live in Yosemite National Park are one population. The black bears that live in Canada are another population. Even though they live in different places, these bears share many traits. They all have fur, four legs, and claws.

▼ The black bears with black fur are found in Maine. Their dark fur helps them stay warm and blend in with their environment.

Animals in different populations do not always look the same. Since populations live in different places, the animals can change in different ways to live in their environments.

▲ Do not be fooled by the name! The black bears that live in Yosemite National Park are brown.

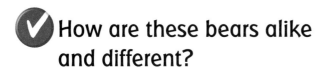 How are these bears alike and different?

▼ Some black bears in Alaska have light fur that helps them hide in the snow.

How can we compare animals in the same population?

Animals in the same population may look and act differently from each other. A meerkat is a small animal that lives in the African desert. Some meerkats are bigger than others. Some are more cautious while others are more curious.

meerkats

Even though meerkats can look and act differently, they share many traits. They all eat insects and grubs. They have long claws for digging and live underground in burrows. They live in large groups and spend time together.

▲ **This meerkat is digging to find insects to eat.**

✔ What other traits do all meerkats have in common?

Think, Talk, and Write

1. **Classify.** Name another animal that you can put in the same group as meerkats.

2. How are black bears in Alaska and California alike and different?

3. Write about an animal with a special trait that helps it live in its environment.

Math Link

Learn about an animal that lives in groups. How many animals are in the group?

Helpful Traits

Animals have traits that help them live in their environments. Ants have powerful jaws that help them bite and carry food. Frogs have strong legs that help them swim and hop.

angler fish

hummingbird

 Write About It

Describe one of the animals above. Where does it live? What do you think it eats? What traits help it live in its environment?

Remember

When you describe, you give details about something.

 e-Journal Write about it online @ **www.macmillanmh.com**

 ELA W 2.1.0. Students write clear and coherent sentences and paragraphs that develop a central idea. Their writing shows they consider the audience and purpose. Students progress through the stages of the writing process (e.g., prewriting, drafting, revising, editing successive versions).

Parts of a Group

This dog had 5 puppies. Even though the puppies share many traits, they look different. In this family, 3 of the 5 puppies are brown. You can write this as the fraction $\frac{3}{5}$.

Write Fractions

How many of the 5 puppies are black? Write a fraction to show your answer.

Now draw a group of 3 puppies. Make one third of the group brown.

Remember

You can use a fraction to tell about parts of a group.

 MA NS 2.4.2. Recognize fractions of a whole and parts of a group (e.g., one-fourth of a pie, two-thirds of 15 balls).

III
EXTEND

Tricky Traits

This fennec fox is only 8 inches tall, but can leap 4 feet!

Why such big ears, you say? They keep the fox cool in the heat of the day. These ears help the fox hear so it can catch its prey. What would you do if you could hear as well as a fox?

The sloth sleeps so much that other animals can live in its fur.

All day long, the sloth hangs upside down in a tree. Its long curved claws wrap easily around branches. The sloth moves so slowly that it is hard to see. Can you move as slowly as the sloth?

Look at this lizard run! What do you think it is running from? The basilisk lizard can skip across water. It has long back legs and large feet. It moves so fast it does not sink. How do you move across water?

Sharks have the strongest jaws on Earth.

Sharks are very good hunters. They can smell food from miles away. They have many rows of sharp teeth to catch their prey. They eat fish, birds, turtles, and seals. How many rows of teeth do you have?

Owls can twist their necks around to see.

The owl's feathers help it fly quietly through the sky. It looks and listens for animals on the ground. It swoops down on them without a sound. Would you like to fly? Why?

When this insect hurts its leg, it can grow a new one!

Is this an insect or a leaf? How can you pick? Walking sticks live in plants and trees. Their shape and color make them hard to see. Birds must find a snack somewhere else! How do you hide?

Vocabulary

larva, page 96   **molting**, page 97

mammal, page 78   **population**, page 106

Use each word once for items 1–4.

1. When a crab hatches from an egg, it is called a _____. 2 LS 2.b

2. A group of animals that live in the same area is called a _____. 2 LS 2.d

3. An animal that has hair or fur and gives birth to live young is a _____. 2 LS 2.b

4. When a grasshopper grows bigger, it sheds its body covering and grows a new one. This is called _____. 2 LS 2.b

5. Communicate. How are the life cycles of a mealworm and a lizard alike and different? 2 LS 2.b

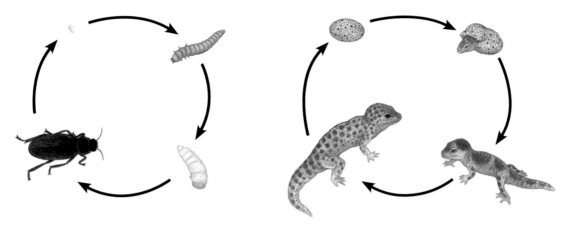

6. Classify. How are these ducklings like their parent? How are they different? 2 LS 2.a

⭐ How do animals grow and change? 2 LS 2.b

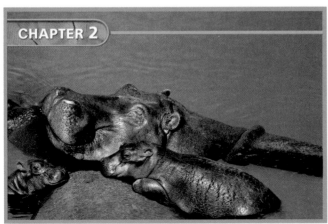

CHAPTER 2

LOG ON ⓔ**-Review** Summaries and quizzes online @ **www.macmillanmh.com**

Get a Clue!

Scientists observe animals and look for clues to help them answer their questions. Look at the pictures. Use clues to answer the questions below.

▶ Which animal group do these animals belong to? How do you know?

▶ What kind of environment do these animals live in?

▶ What parts help them live in their environment?

▶ How do you think these animals stay safe?

2 IE 4.a. Make predictions based on observed patterns and not random guessing.

1 **This picture shows the life cycle of a butterfly.**

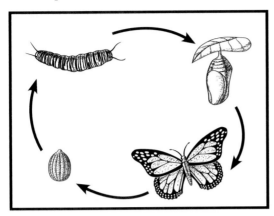

What is the caterpillar called in this life cycle? 2 LS 2.b

A egg

B larva

C pupa

D adult

2 **Why do some black bears have white fur?** 2 LS 2.c

A All black bears are white.

B White fur helps the bears hide in snow.

C White fur keeps the bears cool.

D White fur helps the bears find food.

3 **How is a tiger cub like an adult tiger?** 2 LS 2.a

A They both can hunt for food on their own.

B They both need milk.

C They both can have babies of their own.

D They both have striped fur and claws.

A Frog's Life

Every spring, an amazing thing happens in a pond or lake near you.

It starts when male frogs begin calling. Their loud call tells the female frogs, "Here I am! I am looking for a mate!"

After the frog finds a mate, the female frog lays eggs in the water. The eggs look like balls of jelly with tiny dark spots.

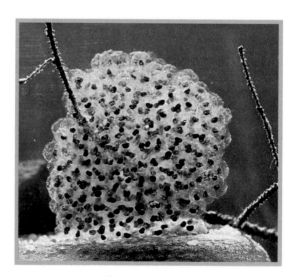

frog eggs

2 LS 2.b. Students know the sequential stages of life cycles are different for different animals, such as butterflies, frogs, and mice.
ELA R 2.2.0. Students read and understand grade-level appropriate material.

Tadpoles hatch from the eggs. A tadpole lives under water. It uses its tail to swim. It eats plants and grows bigger.

tadpole

After a while, the tadpole grows legs. Its tail shrinks. The young frog begins to move to land.

young frog

Finally, the young frog hops out of the water. Its tail is gone. It has turned into an adult frog.

adult frog

Bird Bander

Do you love to learn about birds? You could become a bird bander. A bird bander helps scientists keep track of birds.

The bander catches a bird and puts a tiny band around its ankle. This band has a number on it, and the bander writes it down. The bander also writes the bird's age and size. Then the bander returns the bird to the wild. Later other banders and scientists might trap the same bird. They can look up the bird's number and see how it grew and changed.

bird bander

More Careers to Think About

wildlife guide

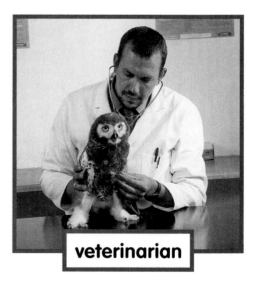

veterinarian

LOG ON e-Careers @ www.macmillanmh.com

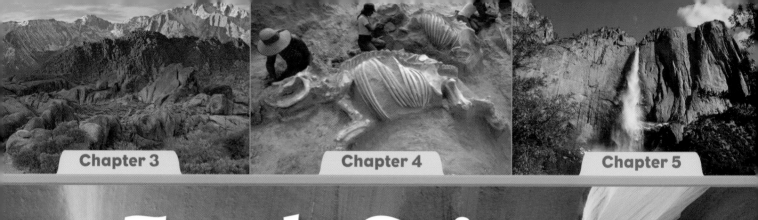

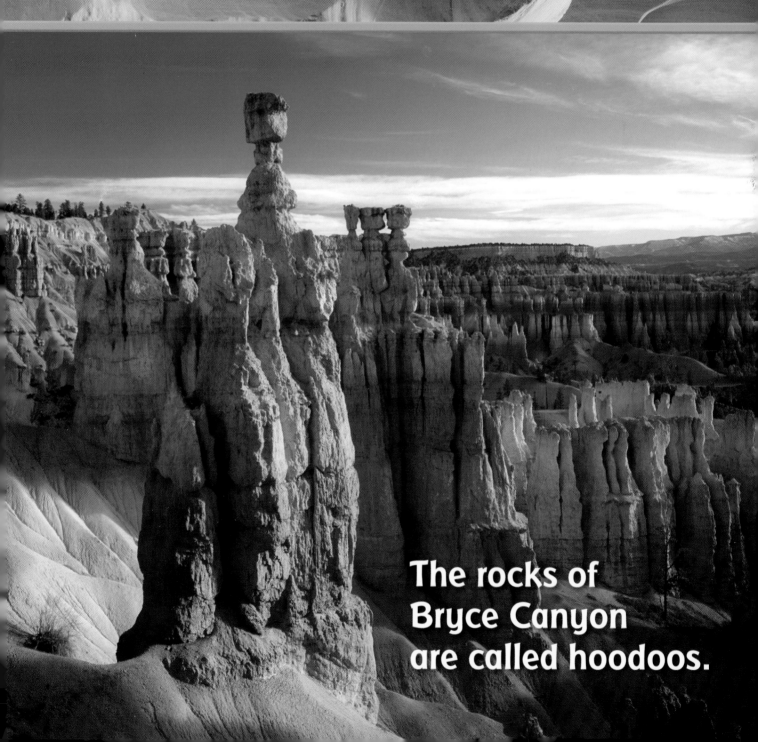

Earth Science

The rocks of
Bryce Canyon
are called hoodoos.

Earth's Materials

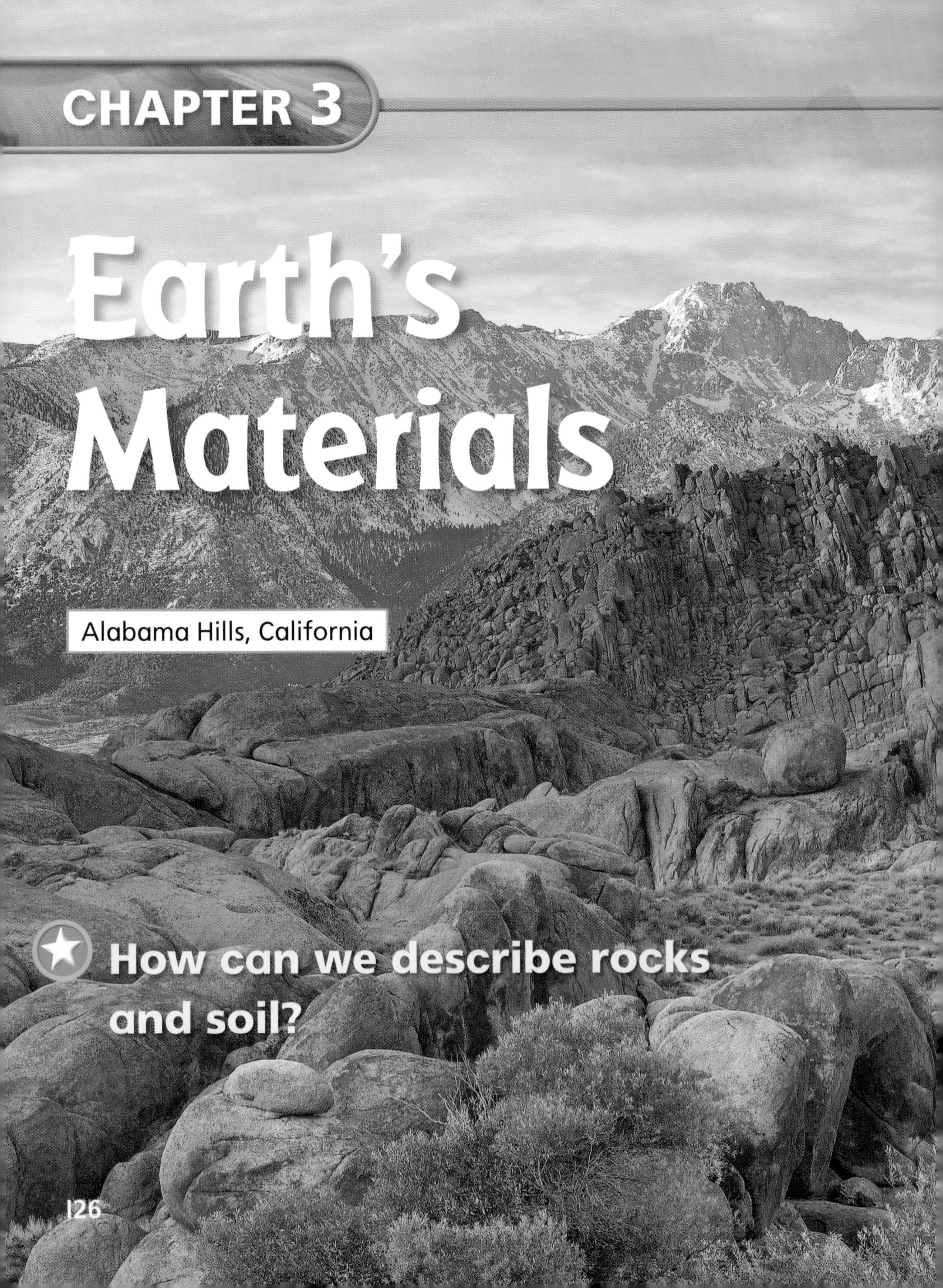

Alabama Hills, California

⭐ How can we describe rocks and soil?

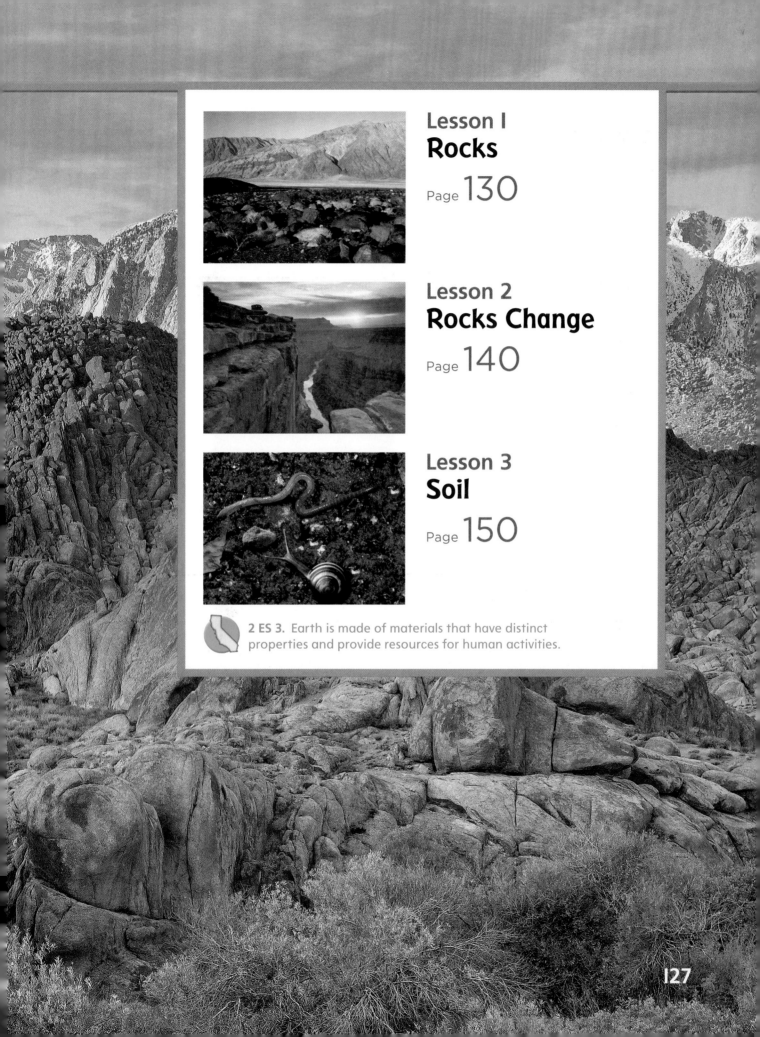

2 ES 3. Earth is made of materials that have distinct properties and provide resources for human activities.

Literature
Poem

ELA R 2.2.0. Students read and understand grade-level appropriate material.

Under a Stone

by Aileen Fisher

In the middle of a meadow
we turned up a stone
and saw a little village
we never had known,
with little streets and tunnels
and ant-folk on the run,
all frightened and excited
by the sudden burst of sun.

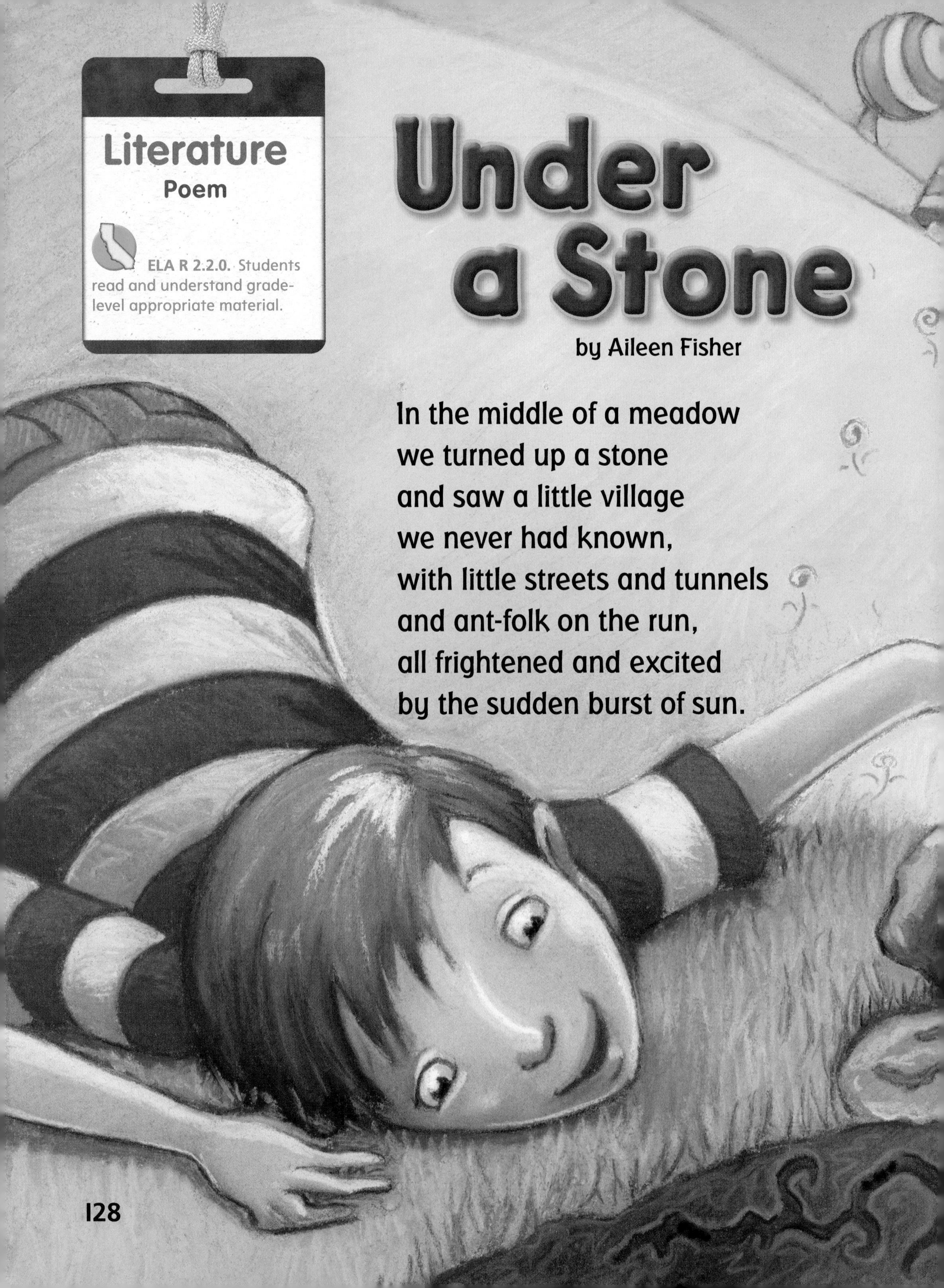

128

We watched them rushing headlong,
and then put back the stone
to cover up the village
we never had known,
to roof away the tunnels
where ants were on the run . . .
before they got all sunburned
in the bright hot sun.

Talk About It

What else could you
find under a rock?

129

Lesson 1
Rocks

Look and Wonder

Have you ever picked up a rock? Scientists do, too. How do you think scientists study rocks?

boulders, Death Valley National Park, California

2 ES 3.a. Students know how to compare the physical properties of different kinds of rocks and know that rock is composed of different combinations of minerals.

Explore

How can we sort rocks?

What to Do

You need

rocks

hand lens

1. **Observe.** Look at your rocks under a hand lens. Describe what you see. How are they alike? How are they different?

2. **Classify.** Put your rocks into groups. Write your groups in a chart. Record how many rocks are in each group.

Explore More

3. **Communicate.** Share your chart with a partner. Discuss how you put the rocks into groups. What other ways can you classify rocks?

Step 2

 2 IE 4.c. Compare and sort common objects according to two or more physical attributes (e.g., color, shape, texture, size, weight).

Vocabulary

geologist

mineral

property

luster

hardness

How can we describe rocks?

A scientist who studies rocks is called a **geologist**. Geologists observe rocks to identify different types. One thing they look at is the color of the rock.

Many rocks are one color. Other rocks are more than one color. Most rocks are gray. Some are black, brown, red, white, or even pink.

▼ **What colors are these rocks?**

gabbro

chalk

basalt

Scientists look at the size of rocks, too. Rocks that are the same size might not weigh the same.

▲ These two rocks are the same size. The pumice weighs less than the malachite.

 What are some things geologists look at when they describe rocks?

mudstone

ironstone

obsidian

pink granite

shale

What are rocks made of?

All rocks are made of **minerals**. Some rocks are made of just one mineral. Other rocks are made of many minerals.

Look at the piece of granite. It is made up of three minerals. The white parts are the mineral feldspar. The gray parts are quartz. The black parts are mica.

▲ Beryl is made of only one mineral.

Minerals in Granite

quartz

feldspar

mica

Read a Diagram

What are the minerals in granite?

Did you know that you use minerals every day? Your pencil is made of the mineral graphite. Plants use the minerals in soil to help them grow. Our bodies need minerals, too. We get minerals from the foods we eat.

fluorite

fluorite mine

▲ **Some toothpastes have fluoride, which is made from the mineral fluorite.**

✔ How do we use minerals?

How can we describe minerals?

A **property** tells you something about an object. Color is one property of a mineral. **Luster** is another. Geologists use the word luster to describe how a mineral looks when light shines on it.

▲ Pyrite's metallic luster tricks some people into thinking it is gold. This mineral is also called fool's gold.

▲ Some minerals, like quartz, shine like glass.

▲ This halloysite does not shine. It has a dull luster.

Another property of a mineral is its **hardness**. Hardness is how tough a rock is. Talc is so soft that you can scratch it with your fingernail. Diamond is so hard that it can only be cut by another diamond.

▲ Talc is the softest mineral.

▲ Diamond is the hardest mineral.

 What are some properties of minerals?

Think, Talk, and Write

1. **Compare and Contrast.** How are diamond and granite alike? How are they different?

2. What are some ways we use minerals?

3. Write about the rocks you see every day.

Art Link

Find different rocks outside. Make a sculpture of them.

Compare

When you **compare**, you look for ways that things are alike and different.

Learn It

Cats meow and have four legs. Dogs bark and have four legs. You can record how cats and dogs are alike and different in a Venn diagram. You write how the animals are alike in the space where the two circles meet.

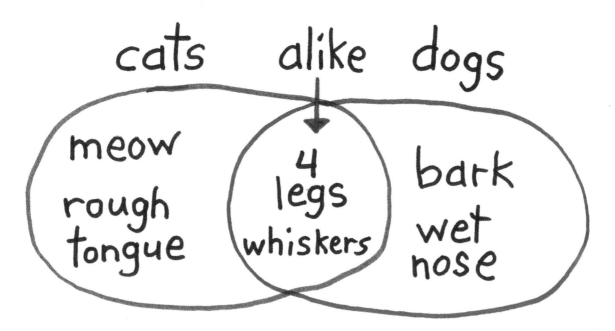

 2 IE 4.c. Compare and sort common objects according to two or more physical attributes (e.g. color, shape, texture, size, weight).

Try It

Look at the pictures below. Then try the skill.

feldspar

quartz

1. How are feldspar and quartz alike? How are they different?

2. Make a Venn diagram to compare feldspar and quartz.

3. **Write About It.** Find two other rocks and compare them. Use a Venn diagram.

Rocks Change

Look and Wonder

How do you think the Grand Canyon was formed? How do you think these rocks changed over time?

 2 ES 3.b. Students know smaller rocks come from the breakage and weathering of larger rocks.

How can you change rocks?

What to Do

You need

rocks

① **Observe.** Look at rocks under a hand lens. Describe what you see.

② **Put the rocks in a jar of water. Shake the jar for two minutes.**

hand lens

Step ②

jar of water

Explore More

③ **Communicate.** Look at the rocks under a hand lens. How did the rocks change?

 2 IE 4.f. Use magnifiers or microscopes to observe and draw descriptions of small objects or small features of objects.

Vocabulary

weathering

SCIENCE QUEST — Explore rocks with the Treasure Hunters.

How do rocks change?

Most rocks are very hard, but did you know that they can change size and shape? The way water and wind change rocks is called **weathering**. When water gets into the cracks of rocks, it can freeze and push against the rocks. The cracks get bigger and then the rocks break.

Beach Rocks

Read a Photo

Look closely at the rocks. What do you think the water is doing to them?

LOG ON — *Science in Motion* Watch how rocks change @ **www.macmillanmh.com**

When rocks slide down a hill, they may break and become smaller. The smaller rocks can then break down into sand. Tiny rocks can become part of the soil.

✓ How does weathering change the shape and size of rocks?

granite arch, Sierra Nevada, California

◀ Strong winds can blow sand against rocks. Wind and sand wore this rock into an arch.

What other ways can rocks change?

Weathering is not the only thing that causes rocks to change. Earthquakes can change rocks, too. When Earth shakes, rocks rub against each other. They can break into smaller pieces.

Plants can also change rocks. Plants can grow in soil inside the cracks of rocks. Sometimes the roots are so strong they cause the rocks to break.

▶ **The roots of this tree have grown into the rock and cracked it.**

You know that rocks are made of minerals. Water can cause some minerals to change.

▲ A rock that has iron will rust in water. It will turn red and brown.

▲ Water caused the copper in this rock to turn green.

 What are some ways rocks can change?

Think, Talk, and Write

1. **Compare and Contrast.** Describe two ways rocks can change.

2. What is weathering?

3. Write about how rocks can become part of soil.

Math Link*

Find rocks outside and sort them into groups. Count how many are in each group.

Rock and Stroll

Rocks are all around us. We see them at the beach and in the mountains. We see them in gardens and on playgrounds. Go for a walk and look at rocks. Take notes about the rocks you see.

 Write About It
Write a letter to a friend. Write about your walk. Describe the rocks you saw. Explain how you think they got their shape.

Remember
A letter shares news with someone.

 e-Journal Write about it online @ **www.macmillanmh.com**

 ELA W 2.2.2. Write a friendly letter complete with the date, salutation, body, closing, and signature.

Rock Patterns

You can use rocks to make patterns. Look at the pattern below. What kind of rock do you think would come next? How do you know?

Make a Pattern

Use rocks or draw pictures of rocks to make a pattern. Share it with a partner. Have your partner explain what rock they think will come next.

Remember
A pattern has a unit that repeats.

MA SDAP 2.2.0. Students demonstrate an understanding of patterns and how patterns grow and describe them in general ways.

Rocks Rule!

Geologists at the American Museum of Natural History travel all around the world to collect rocks. There are thousands of rocks in the museum. Some rocks are just like the ones you might find in a park. Other rocks are rare and strange!

Geologists use different tools to observe rocks. They use a rock hammer to break open a stone. Then they use a hand lens to observe what is inside. They look at the minerals that make up rocks. Scientists can see how the rocks were formed. They can find out where the rocks came from. Geologists can tell if the rocks came from a beach or a volcano.

▲ Some rocks that come from a beach are smooth.

▲ Azurite is a rare rock.

hand lens

rock hammer

ELA R 2.2.5. Restate facts and details in the text to clarify and organize ideas.

▶ **This geologist is using a rock hammer.**

Talk About It

Compare and Contrast. How are a beach rock and azurite alike and different?

LOG ON e**-Journal** Write about it online @ **www.macmillanmh.com**

AMERICAN
MUSEUM of
NATURAL
HISTORY

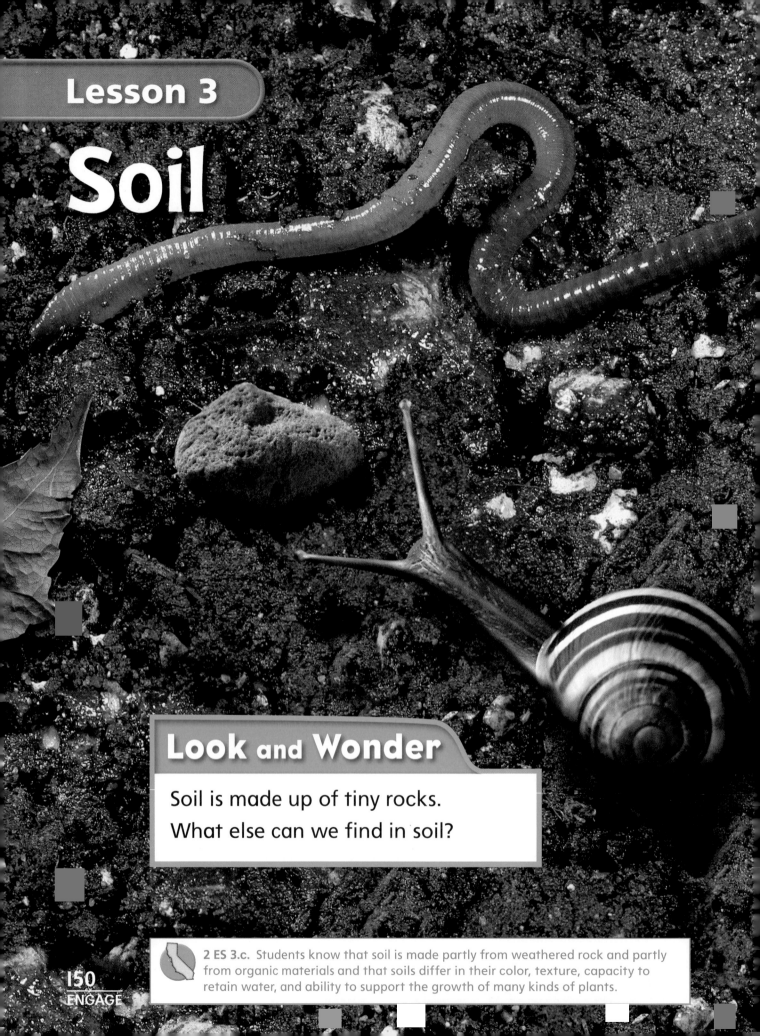

Soil

Look and Wonder

Soil is made up of tiny rocks.
What else can we find in soil?

2 ES 3.c. Students know that soil is made partly from weathered rock and partly from organic materials and that soils differ in their color, texture, capacity to retain water, and ability to support the growth of many kinds of plants.

Explore

What is in soil?

What to Do

1 Put some soil in a strainer. Gently shake it over a plate.

Step **1**

2 **Observe.** Look at the soil on the plate. Use a hand lens. Draw what you see.

3 Pour the soil in the strainer on to another plate. Observe the soil. Draw what you see.

Explore More

4 **Draw a Conclusion.** What is in this soil?

You need

soil

strainer

paper plates

hand lens

 2 IE 4.f. Use magnifiers or microscopes to observe and draw descriptions of small objects or small features of objects.

Vocabulary

soil

What is in soil?

Soil is made of tiny rocks and bits of plants and animals. Weathering makes large rocks break down into smaller rocks. They become part of the soil. When plants and animals die, they begin to rot. They break down and go into the soil.

Soil

Read a Diagram

What is in this soil?

Most plants grow in soil. Plants take in minerals from the soil to grow. People and animals need minerals to grow, too. One of the ways we get minerals is by eating plants that have grown in soil.

 How do people use soil?

corn field, Central Valley, California

What are some kinds of soil?

Did you know that there are different kinds of soil? Some soils are red. Other soils are dark brown or black. The minerals in the rocks give these soils their color.

◀ This clay soil gets its red color from iron. Clay soil does not take in much water.

◀ Sandy soil is light brown. This kind of soil does not hold much water.

Most plants grow best in topsoil. There are many nutrients in topsoil. Some plants grow best in sandy soil. Sand keeps the soil from getting too wet. Some plants grow best in a mix of topsoil and sandy soil.

 What are some ways that soils are alike and different?

▼ **Topsoil is dark brown or black. It has bits of dead animals and plants in it. Topsoil can hold a lot of water.**

How do animals help soil?

Animals that live in the soil help make the soil better for the plants that grow in it. Ants, worms, gophers, and other animals live underground. They make tunnels in the soil. When they dig, they mix the soil. This helps air and water get into the soil.

When animals die, their bodies break down. They become part of the soil. Nutrients in the soil from dead plants and animals help new plants grow.

▲ Gophers dig tunnels and mix the soil.

How do animals help the soil?

Think, Talk, and Write

1. **Compare and Contrast.** How are topsoil and sandy soil alike? How are they different? Make a Venn diagram.

2. What makes some soils red?

3. Write about how animals help soil.

Art L*ink

Make a collage of different animals that live in the soil.

Be a Scientist

You need

2 cups

sand

topsoil

seeds

measuring cup

Which soil is better for growing plants?

Find out the kinds of soil plants need.

What to Do

1. **Measure.** Fill one cup with I cup of sand. Mix the soil. Label the cup Sand.

2. **Measure.** Fill another cup with I cup of topsoil. Label this cup Soil.

2 IE 4.b. Measure length, weight, temperature, and liquid volume with appropriate tools and express those measurements in standard metric system units.

3 **Observe.** Plant a seed in each cup. Put water in each cup. Observe how each plant grows.

Step 3

Sand   Soil

4 **Draw a Conclusion.** What happened to the seed in each cup? Which soil is better for growing plants?

Investigate More

Predict. What will happen if you plant a seed in a mix of sand and soil?

Rocks on the Move

Did you know that rocks can move? Many rocks start at the top of a mountain. Water fills cracks in big mountain rocks. The water freezes, and the ice pushes against the sides of the cracks. Pieces of big rocks break off.

When rocks break and fall, they hit other rocks and break some more. Melting snow carries these rocks into rivers. The rocks can move far away to new places.

In the rivers, rocks bump into each other. More little pieces break off. The rocks get smaller and smoother. Some of these rocks end up next to the river.

Some little pieces of rock mix with pieces of dead plants and animals to become soil. Plants use this soil to grow.

Some rocks travel all the way to the ocean. The rocks bump into each other when waves crash on the shore. More little pieces break off and become sand.

Some sand is just one color, because it is made of the same type of rock. Some sand is many colors because it is made of different kinds of rocks. It takes thousands of years for mountain rocks to become sand.

Vocabulary

luster, page 136

minerals, page 134

properties, page 136

soil, page 152

weathering, page 142

Use each word once for items 1–5.

1. The way water and wind change rocks is called _____. 2 ES 3.c

2. All rocks are made of _____. 2 ES 3.a

3. Tiny rocks and pieces of dead plants and animals are in _____. 2 ES 3.c

4. The way a mineral looks under light is its _____. 2 ES 3.a

5. This mineral is very hard and shines under light. Those are its _____. 2 ES 3.a

6. How do rocks become part of the soil? 2 ES 3.b

7. Describe three properties of this rock. 2 ES 3.a

8. Compare. In what ways can water and plants change rocks? 2 ES 3.b

 How can we describe rocks and soil? 2 ES 3.c

CHAPTER 3

Make a Book

Make a book about how rocks change.

▶ Think about four ways rocks can change.

▶ Write this sentence on four pages:
   _____ can change rocks.

▶ Draw a picture on each page to show what makes rocks change.

▶ Put the pages together to make a book.

2 ES 3.b. Students know smaller rocks come from the breakage and weathering of larger rocks.

1 **How do worms help soil?** 2 ES 3.c

   A They make the soil dry.

   B They give the soil its color.

   C They build tunnels and mix the soil.

   D They turn rocks into food for other animals.

2 **This picture shows a rock.**

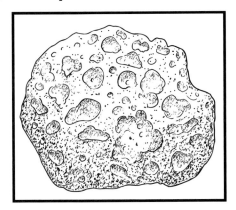

What property can you see in this rock? 2 ES 3.a

   A hardness

   B roughness

   C luster

   D minerals

3 **How can wind change rocks?** 2 ES 3.b

   A Wind can make rocks bigger.

   B Wind can blow sand against rocks and wear them down.

   C Wind can cause water to freeze inside rocks.

   D Wind can cause rocks to change color.

CHAPTER 4

Earth's Past

⭐ **What can fossils tell us about Earth's past?**

 2 ES 3. Earth is made of materials that have distinct properties and provide resources for human activities.

171

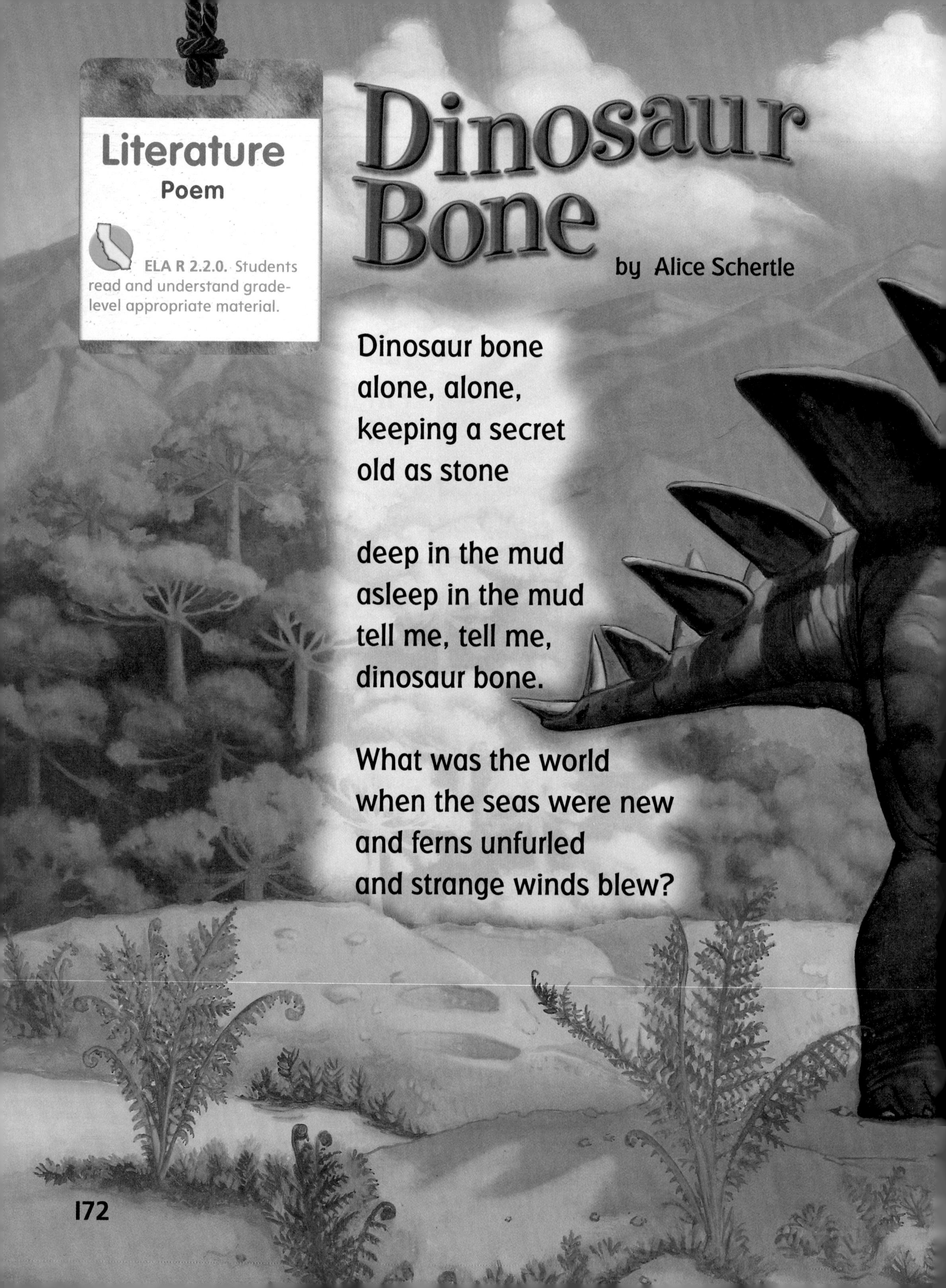

Literature

Poem

ELA R 2.2.0. Students read and understand grade-level appropriate material.

Dinosaur Bone

by Alice Schertle

Dinosaur bone
alone, alone,
keeping a secret
old as stone

deep in the mud
asleep in the mud
tell me, tell me,
dinosaur bone.

What was the world
when the seas were new
and ferns unfurled
and strange winds blew?

Were the mountains fire?
Were the rivers ice?
Was it mud and mire?
Was it paradise?

How did it smell,
your earth, your sky?
How did you live?
How did you die?

How long have you lain
alone, alone?
Tell me, tell me,
dinosaur bone.

Talk About It

What do you think a
dinosaur bone can tell
about a dinosaur?

Fossils

Look and Wonder

Look at these fossil prints. What kind of animal do you think made them? How do you know?

 2 ES 3.d. Students know that fossils provide evidence about the plants and animals that lived long ago and that scientists learn about the past history of Earth by studying fossils.

Explore

How can we get clues from prints?

What to Do

You need

small objects

1. Press a secret object into clay. Gently take the object away.

2. **Observe.** Trade clay prints with a partner. Look at the print under a hand lens.

clay

3. **Infer.** What object do you think made the print? Draw a picture.

Explore More

hand lens

4. **Communicate.** What clues did you use to figure out what made the print?

 2 IE 4.f. Use magnifiers or microscopes to observe and draw descriptions of small objects or small features of objects.

Step 1

Vocabulary

fossil

 Explore fossils with the Treasure Hunters.

What are fossils?

A **fossil** is what is left of a living thing from the past. Some fossils are bones or teeth of animals that lived long ago. Other fossils are prints of whole plants and animals. Fossils help us see what life was like long ago.

▶ These Therizinosaurus eggs were found in China.

◀ A fern left a print in this rock.

Scientists find fossils of plants and animals in many places. Some are found in rock. Others can be found in ice, tar, or amber. Amber is a sticky liquid in trees that has become hard. Sometimes plants or insects were trapped in the amber and became fossils.

▲ This insect got trapped in amber millions of years ago.

✔ Where can scientists find fossils of plants and animals?

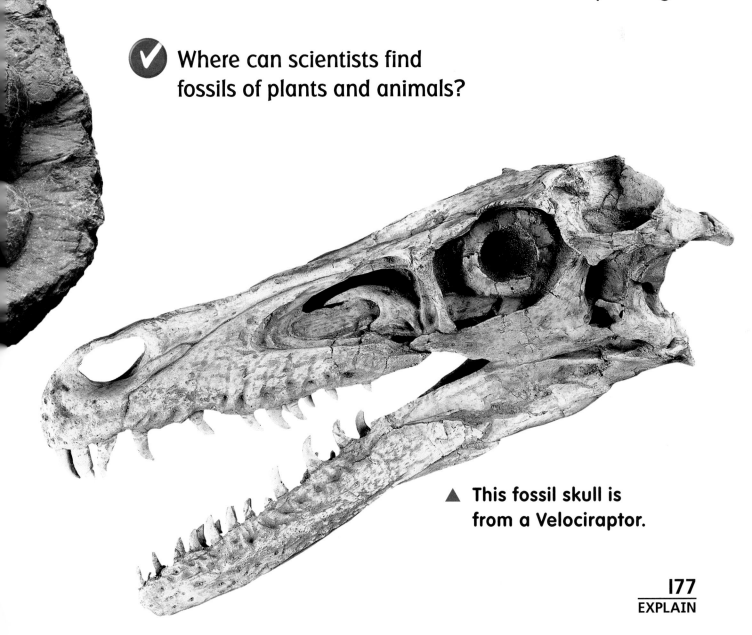

▲ This fossil skull is from a Velociraptor.

How do fossils form?

Fossils form when living things are buried under many layers of sand or mud. Scientists can tell how old a fossil is by looking at the layers. Some fossils are found in the same layer. This means that those plants and animals lived at about the same time.

▶ **This fossil is a claw of a raptor.**

 How can scientists find out how old a fossil is?

How a Fossil Forms

① **A raptor dies. It is buried in sediment, like mud, clay, and soil.**

② **More sediment builds up. The soft parts of the raptor rot away.**

Think, Talk, and Write

1. **Sequence.** How are fossils formed?

2. What is a fossil?

3. Write about where fossils can be found.

Music Link*

Write a song about finding a fossil.

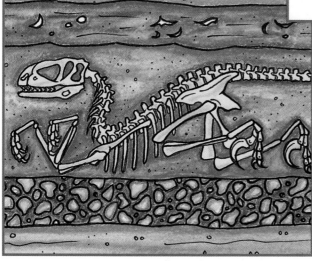

③ **Minerals replace the bones and teeth, and they slowly harden into rock.**

Read a Diagram

What happens to the bones and teeth of the raptor?

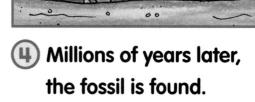

LOG ON *Science in Motion* Watch how fossils form @ **www.macmillanmh.com**

④ **Millions of years later, the fossil is found.**

Sequence

A **sequence** tells the order in which things happen. A sequence tells what happens first, next, and last.

▲ **A seedling grows.**

Learn It

Think about how a plant grows. Then look at the pictures and put them in order. You can use a chart to help you tell the sequence.

◀ **The plant gets bigger.**

▲ **I plant a seed.**

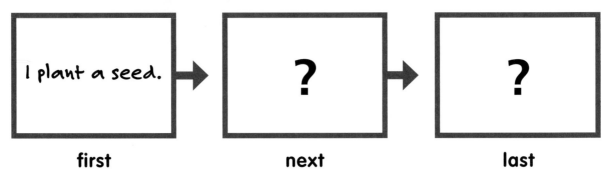

I plant a seed.	→	?	→	?
first		**next**		**last**

  2 IE 4.d. Write or draw descriptions of a sequence of steps, events, and observations.

Try It

Look at the pictures. Then try the skill.

▲ **fossil fern**

▲ **buried fern**

▲ **fern**

1. Which picture comes first? Next? Last?

2. What happened to the fern?

3. Write About It. How do fossils form?

Life of a Dinosaur

Do you have a favorite dinosaur? Learn about one from a book or on the Internet.

Write About It

Write a report about your dinosaur. Tell where the dinosaur lived and how it moved. What did it eat? Draw a picture of your dinosaur. Share your report with the class.

Remember

A report gives many details about a topic.

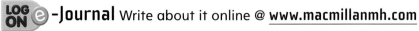

LOG ON **e -Journal** Write about it online @ **www.macmillanmh.com**

 ELA W 2.2.0. Students write compositions that describe and explain familiar objects, events, and experiences. Student writing demonstrates a command of standard American English and the drafting, research, and organizational strategies outlined in Writing Standard 1.0.

Measuring Dinosaurs

How long were dinosaurs? Scientists can study fossils to find out. This chart shows the length of some dinosaurs.

Dinosaur Lengths

Dinosaur		Length
Compsognathus		100 centimeters
Archaeopteryx		30 centimeters
Protoceratops		200 centimeters

Use a Ruler

Look at the dinosaur lengths. Use a centimeter ruler to measure string in the same lengths. Then lay the string on the floor. Now measure the length of each dinosaur in your footsteps.

Remember

You can measure to find out how long something is.

MA MG 2.1.1. Measure the length of objects by iterating (repeating) a nonstandard or standard unit.

Finding Clues in Fossils

Look and Wonder

What do you think this animal looked like when it was alive?

2 ES 3.d. Students know that fossils provide evidence about the plants and animals that lived long ago and that scientists learn about the past history of Earth by studying fossils.

What clues can you find in this fossil?

What to Do

1. **Observe.** Look at the picture of the fossil.

2. **Infer.** Draw a picture of what this animal might have looked like.

Explore More

Step **3**

3. **Infer.** Look at the feet. How do you think this animal moved? Why?

Vocabulary

paleontologist

extinct

skeleton

How can fossils help us learn about the past?

A **paleontologist** is a scientist who studies fossils. The fossils give clues about what Earth was like long ago. For example, animal fossils tell about what kinds of animals roamed Earth. These fossils also tell about what the land might have looked like.

Paleontologists found this fish fossil in a dry place in Wyoming.

By studying fossils, paleontologists have learned that the weather was different millions of years ago. In Antarctica, scientists have found plant fossils under the ice. These plant fossils look like plants that grow in warm places today. Paleontologists can infer that the weather there used to be warm.

▲ **This scientist is digging in Antarctica.**

 What can scientists learn from fossils?

Palm Frond Fossil

Read a Photo

What does this fossil tell you about how this place has changed?

What can fossils teach us about extinct animals?

When a living thing is **extinct**, it has died out. None of its kind is living anywhere on Earth. Some plants and animals become extinct because of disease. Sometimes big changes on Earth make plants and animals die out.

▼ **This mammoth's head was found in the ice. The ice kept many parts of the head from rotting away.**

Paleontologists learn about extinct animals. They find fossil bones and put them together. They can make a **skeleton**, or a full set of bones. Scientists can learn about the animal's size. They can tell how it may have moved.

▲ **This scientist is cleaning the mammoth fossil.**

 What can scientists learn from an animal skeleton?

Think, Talk, and Write

1. **Sequence.** How do paleontologists find fossils and then learn from them?

2. How can scientists learn about the weather long ago?

3. Write about why animals might become extinct.

Art Link

Make a diorama of a dinosaur fossil. Show the place where it was found.

You need

clay

leaves

plastic knife

hand lens

How do clues help scientists put fossils together?

Find out how scientists put fossils together.

What to Do

1. Work in a small group. Roll out some clay and press a leaf into it. Peel it off carefully.

2 IE 4.c. Compare and sort two objects according to two or more physical attributes.

2 Cut your leaf print into two pieces. You do not have to use straight lines.

3 Trade your leaf prints with another group.

Step 2

4 **Infer.** Use clues in the prints to match them and put them together.

Step 4

Investigate More

Communicate. How would you put together a dinosaur? How did this activity help you learn how palentologists work?

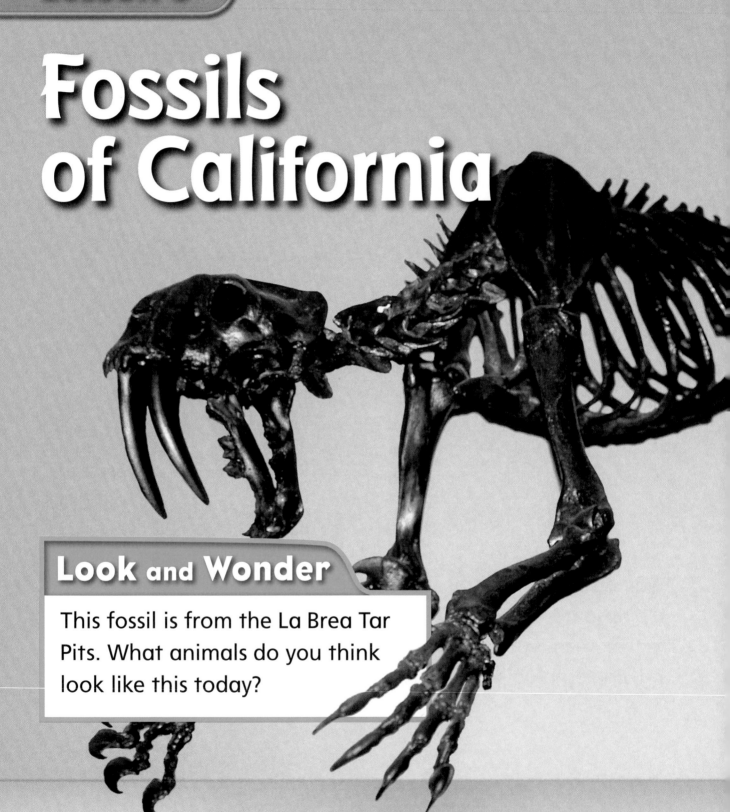

Fossils of California

Look and Wonder

This fossil is from the La Brea Tar Pits. What animals do you think look like this today?

2 ES 3.d. Students know that fossils provide evidence about the plants and animals that lived long ago and that scientists learn about the past history of Earth by studying fossils.

How do animal fossils compare to animals today?

What to Do

1. **Observe.** Look at the fossil of the saber-toothed cat. Describe what you see.

2. Look at the picture of the cat. Describe what you see.

Step 2

Explore More

3. **Compare.** How are the animals alike? How are they different? Make a Venn diagram to compare.

What are the La Brea Tar Pits?

At Rancho La Brea in California, thick asphalt comes up from the Earth. The asphalt is black and sticky, just like tar. Scientists have found about 3 million fossils of plants and animals in the pits. Some of the fossils are about 40,000 years old.

▲ **This scientist is taking fossils out of the tar pits.**

▼ **Rancho La Brea has models of the mammoths that were trapped in the tar pits.**

Scientists think that the weather used to be humid and warm because they have found fossils of frogs and turtles. Palentologists have also found fossils of seeds, leaves, and cones.

Today asphalt still comes up from Earth and plants and animals get trapped in the pits. They could become fossils many years from now.

✓ **What fossils have scientists found in the tar?**

What other fossils are found in California?

The Lambeosaurus was a duck-billed dinosaur that lived 76 million years ago. Its fossils were found in Baja California, a part of Mexico. It had a bony crest on its head. It ate plants with its flat teeth.

The Ankylosaur was short and covered with bony plates. It lived about 100 million years ago. Scientists found its fossils in Carlsbad, California. It also ate plants.

Lambeosaurus

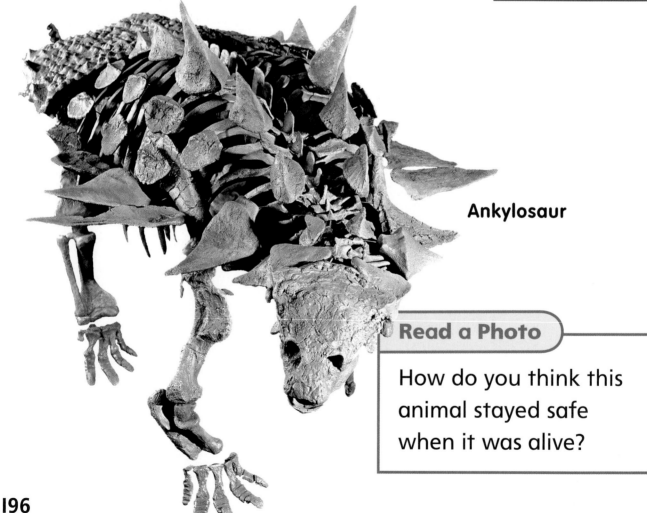

Ankylosaur

Read a Photo

How do you think this animal stayed safe when it was alive?

Another type of fossil is petrified wood. Trees that are covered by water, mud, and ash slowly turn to stone. Even though they are rocks, the trees still look like wood. Scientists can observe the rings in petrified wood to tell how old it is.

▲ **Petrified wood is found in many parts of California.**

 What can we learn from fossils?

Think, Talk, and Write

1. **Sequence.** Explain how trees become petrified.

2. What animals lived in California long ago?

3. Write about why you think some animals do not live here anymore.

Art Link

Learn about a fossil found in California. Make a poster and share it with your classmates.

Meet Mike Novacek

Mike Novacek grew up in Southern California. When he was young he visited the La Brea Tar Pits in Los Angeles. He loved to learn about the fossils he saw there. He learned about animals that lived long ago.

Mike Novacek

▼ **Mike travels to the Gobi Desert in China to look for new fossils.**

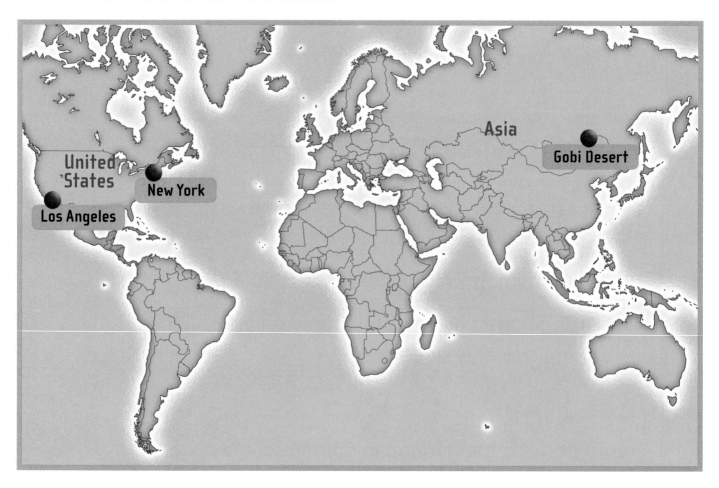

ELA R 2.2.4. Ask clarifying questions about essential textual elements of exposition (e.g., *why, what if, how*).

Today Mike is a scientist at the American Museum of Natural History in New York. He travels all around the world to collect fossils of reptiles, mammals, and dinosaurs. Many of these animals lived 80 million years ago!

Mike and his team went to the Gobi Desert to look for fossils. They found fossils of the Kryptobaatar, which are tiny mammals the size of mice. These mammals lived at the same time and place as dinosaurs!

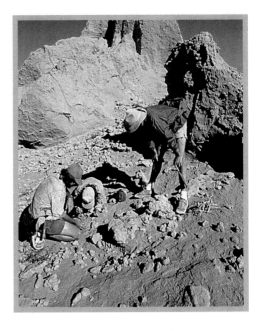

▲ Mike studies fossils to find out about Earth's past.

◄ Kryptobaatar skull

Talk About It

Classify. How can you put fossils into groups?

LOG ON e-Journal Write about it online @ www.macmillanmh.com

AMERICAN MUSEUM OF NATURAL HISTORY

Found Fossils

Sometimes scientists find fossils in surprising places. These paleontologists are digging for fossils in Wyoming. Today this place is cold and dry. What fossils might they find?

Paleontologists found all of these
fossils in the desert in Wyoming! Do
you think these kinds of animals live in
Wyoming today? Why or why not?

These fossils are clues to the past.
They help us learn what this place
was like long ago. What do you think
Wyoming looked like when the fish
lived there?

When the fish lived here there was water! This is what Wyoming might have looked like long ago. Scientists know that the environment used to be warmer and wetter.

Which plants and animals look like
the fossils the paleontologists found?
What other animals do you think
could have lived here?

Vocabulary

extinct, page 188	**paleontologist**, page 186
fossil, page 176	**skeleton**, page 189

Use each word once for items 1–4.

1. A _____ is a print or part of a living thing left from the past. 2 ES 3.d

2. A full set of bones like this one is called a _____. 2 ES 3.d

3. When a living thing dies out and no more of its kind are left, it is_____. 2 ES 3.d

4. A _____ is a scientist who studies fossils. 2 ES 3.d

5. **Sequence.** Explain how a fossil forms. 2 ES 3.d

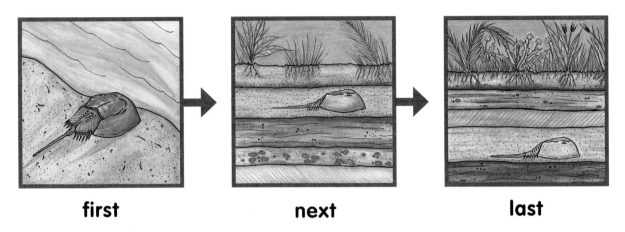

first   next   last

6. How can scientists learn about extinct animals? 2 ES 3.d

7. What are some fossils that have been found in California? 2 ES 3.d

⭐ What can fossils tell us about Earth's past? 2 ES 3.d

CHAPTER 4

Be a Paleontologist!

Scientists found these fossils in the desert.
They were in the same layer of rock.

▶ **What kinds of plants and animals lived in this place long ago?**

▶ **What do you think the weather was like?**

▶ **What do you think this place looked like long ago? Draw a picture or make a model of it.**

2 ES 3.d. Students know that fossils provide evidence about the plants and animals that lived long ago and that scientists learn about the past history of Earth by studying fossils.

1 **What can make plants and animals die out?** 2 ES 3.d

   A big changes on Earth

   B warm weather

   C weathering of rocks

   D too much food

2 **The picture below shows a dinosaur fossil.**

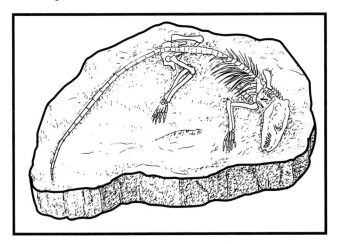

How do you think this animal moved when it was alive? 2 ES 3.d

   A swam in water

   B flew in air

   C slid across the ground

   D walked on four legs

3 **What can we learn by looking at fossil feet?** 2 ES 3.d

   A how the animal moved

   B what the animal ate

   C what color the animal was

   D why the animal died

Earth's Resources

⭐ How do we use
Earth's resources?

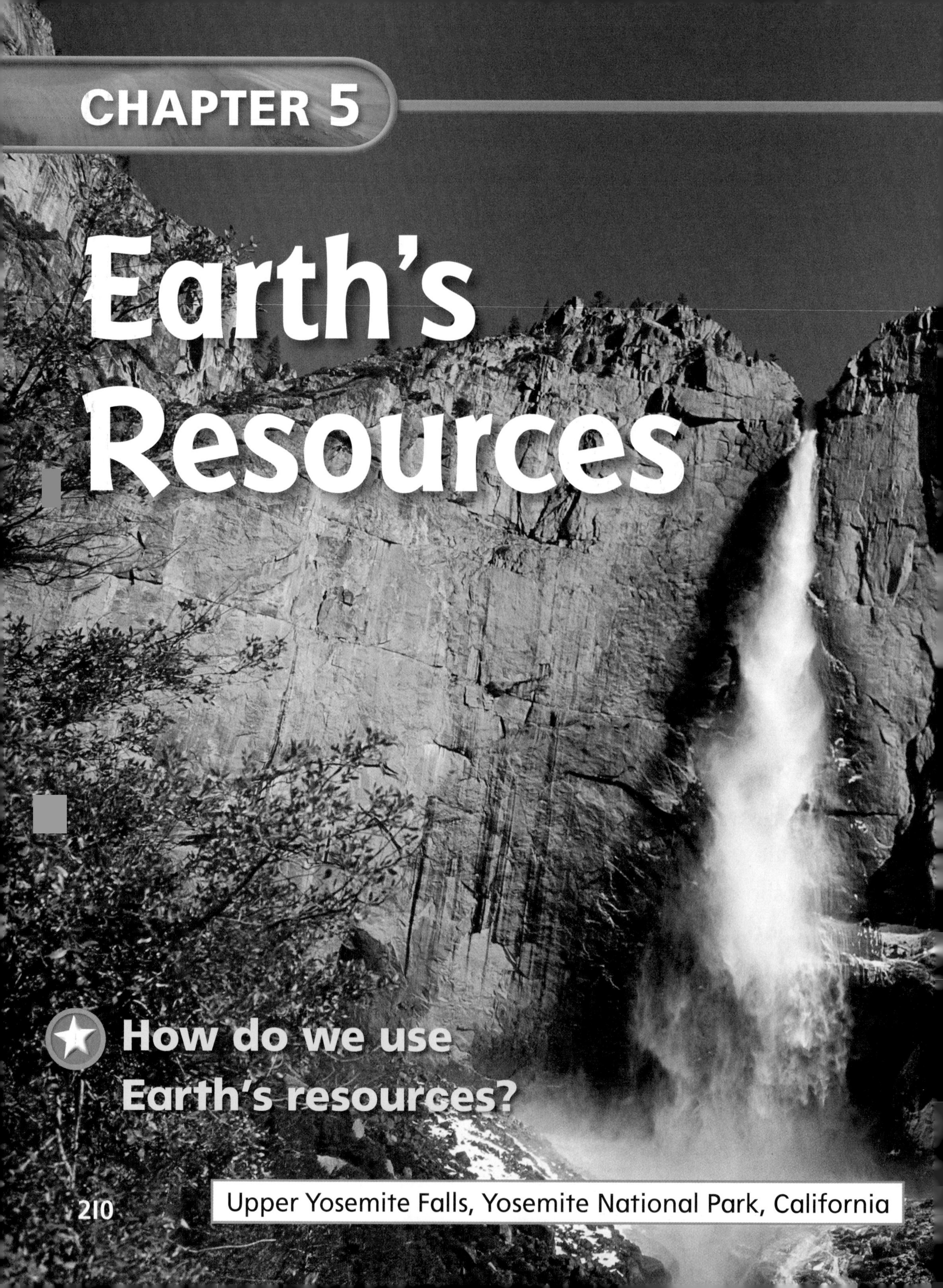

Upper Yosemite Falls, Yosemite National Park, California

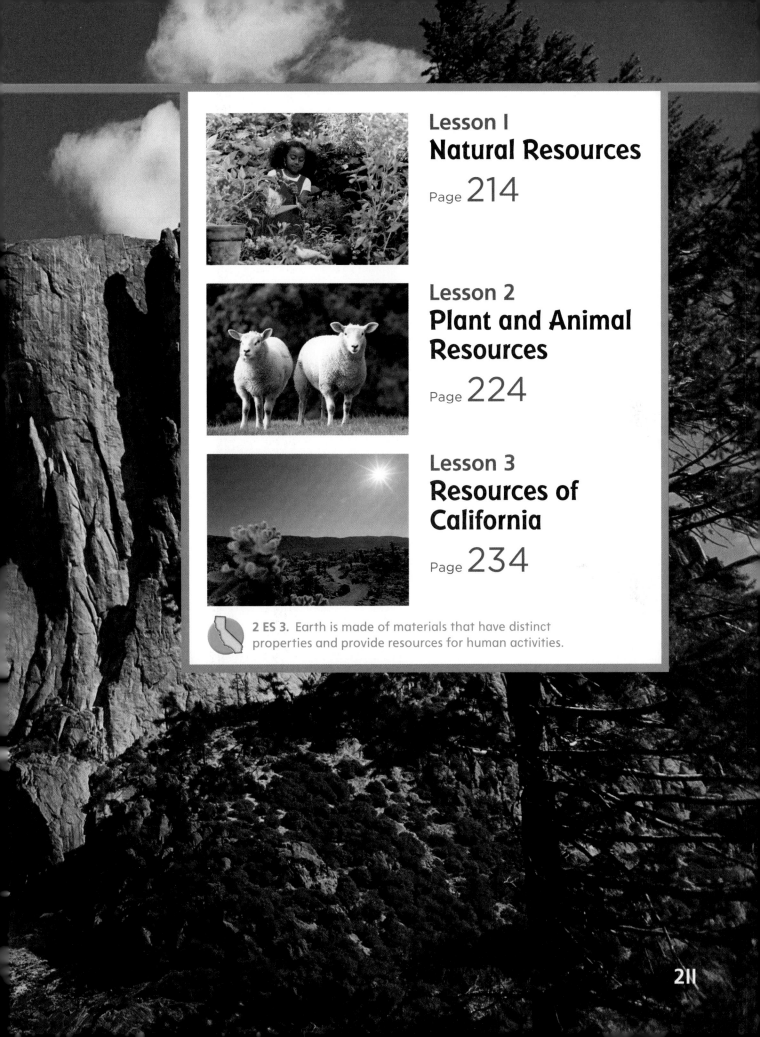

2 ES 3. Earth is made of materials that have distinct properties and provide resources for human activities.

Literature
Poem

ELA R 2.2.0. Students read and understand grade-level appropriate material.

Sun

by Valerie Worth

The Sun
Is a leaping fire
Too hot
To go near.

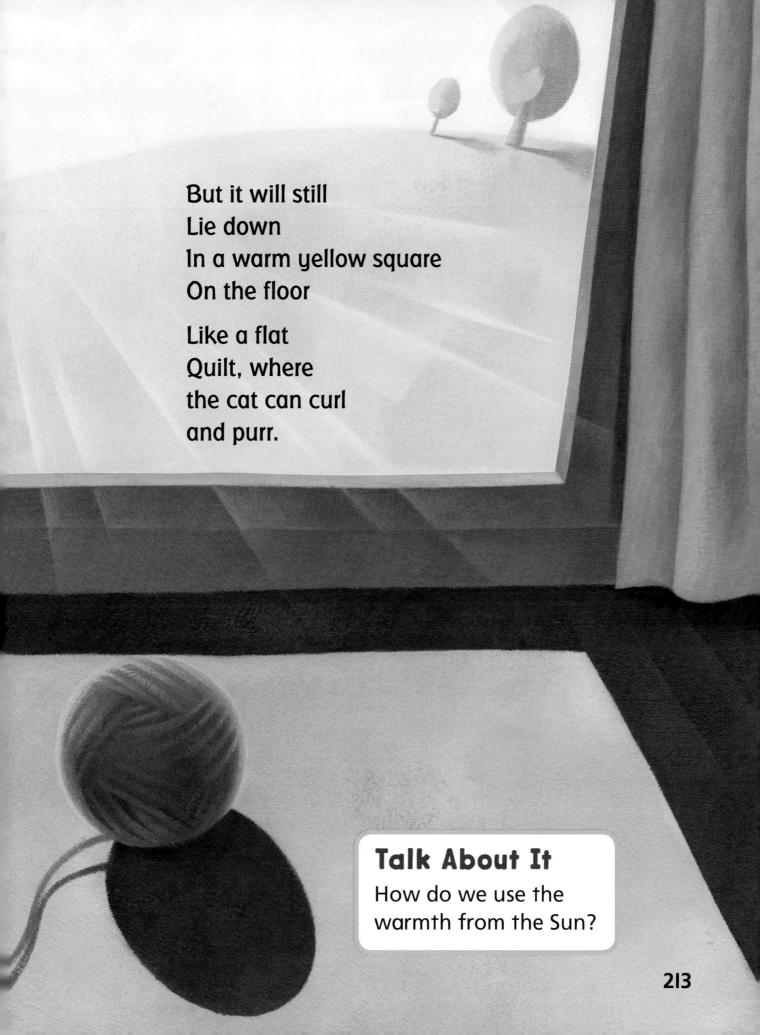

But it will still
Lie down
In a warm yellow square
On the floor

Like a flat
Quilt, where
the cat can curl
and purr.

Talk About It

How do we use the
warmth from the Sun?

Natural Resources

Look and Wonder

All living things need water.
How do we use water every day?

 2 ES 3.e. Students know rock, water, plants, and soil provide many resources, including food, fuel, and building materials, that humans use.

What ways do you use water?

What to Do

1. **Record Data.** How many times do you use water during the day?

2. How many times did you drink water? What other ways did you use water? Make a tally chart.

3. Use your tally chart to make a bar graph. Show how many times you used water.

Explore More

4. **Communicate.** What ways do you use water at home?

How I Use Water

drink water	III
wash hands	

2 IE 4.e. Construct bar graphs to record data, using appropriately labeled axes.

What are natural resources?

A **natural resource** is something from Earth that people use. Rocks, minerals, plants, soil, and water are natural resources. What are some other natural resources?

▼ People use things from nature to live.

We use natural resources to make things we use every day. Your shirt might be made of cotton, which comes from a plant. Your desk might be made out of wood. Take a look at this pencil. What natural resources were used to make it?

 What other things are made of wood?

Pencil

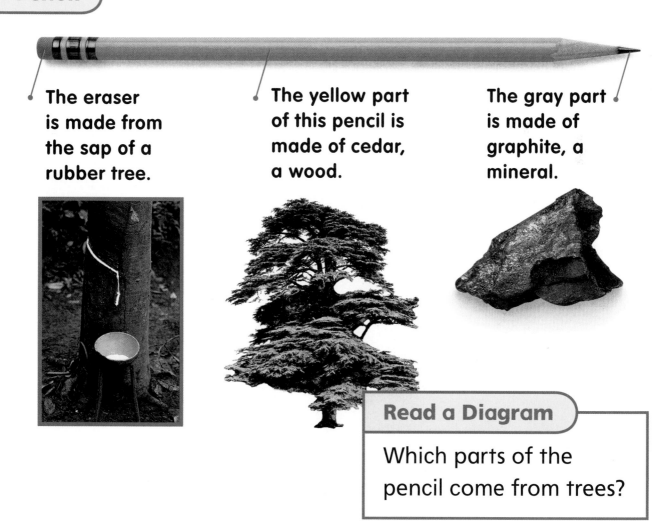

The eraser is made from the sap of a rubber tree.

The yellow part of this pencil is made of cedar, a wood.

The gray part is made of graphite, a mineral.

Read a Diagram

Which parts of the pencil come from trees?

How do we use rocks and soil?

Rocks and soil are natural resources. You know that we need rocks and soil to live. Rocks break down and become part of the soil. Plants use the soil to grow. We need plants for food and to make things such as paper and clothes.

▼ **These corn plants need rocks and soil to grow.**

We also use rocks to build homes. Concrete is made by mixing rocks, sand, and water. We use concrete to make buildings and sidewalks. We use the minerals in sand to make glass. We use minerals to make jewelry, too. We even eat some minerals.

✓ Why are rocks and soil important?

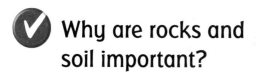
Salt is a mineral that we eat.

The blue parts of this bracelet are turquoise, a mineral.

▼ This building is made with rocks.

How do we use water and wind?

Water and wind are natural resources, too. We use water to drink, cook, and clean. We use water to grow plants. We also use water for energy. We can use moving water to make electric power. This power lights and heats homes.

▼ **Turbines inside the dam make electric power.**

▼ **The water that moves over the dam has a lot of force. We can use this force.**

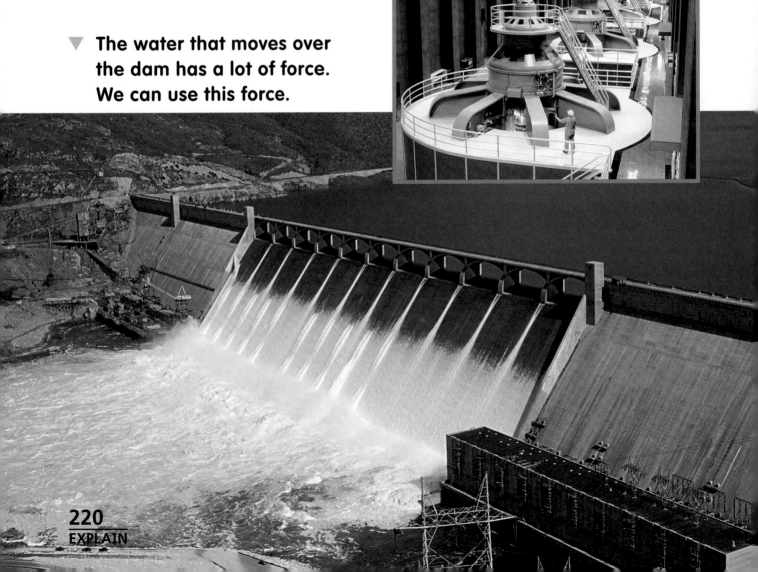

▲ **These windmills go around and around to make electric power.**

Have you ever seen a sailboat move across the water or a flag wave in the wind? Then you know that wind can make things move. Like water, wind can also make electric power.

 In what other ways do you use water and wind?

Think, Talk, and Write

1. Summarize. What are some natural resources?

2. How do people use rocks?

3. What do you think is our most important natural resource? Why?

Art Link

Use rocks and glue to make a sculpture.

Record Data

When you **record data**, you write down information in a chart.

Learn It

How many dogs and cats do students in your class have? You can record the numbers in a tally chart. Then you can use the tally chart to make a bar graph. You can compare the number of cats and dogs.

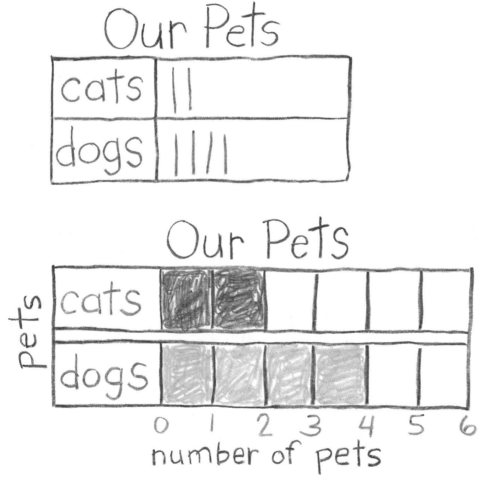

2 IE 4.e. Construct bar graphs to record data, using appropriately labeled axes.

Try It

Look around your classroom. Find objects made out of plants. Find objects made out of minerals. Record what you find in a tally chart and a bar graph.

1. How many objects made out of plants did you find?

2. How many objects made out of minerals did you find?

3. **Write About It.** Why is a bar graph useful?

Plant and Animal Resources

Look and Wonder

How do we use the wool from these sheep?

2 ES 3.e. Students know rock, water, plants, and soil provide many resources, including food, fuel, and building materials, that humans use.

How do we use plants and animals?

What to Do

1. **Observe.** What are you wearing today? What clothes are made from plants?

2. Look at your shoes. What parts are made from animals? What parts are made from plants?

Explore More

3. **Observe.** Look around the room. What things are made from plants? What things are made from animals? How do you know?

 2 IE 4.d. Write or draw descriptions of a sequence of steps, events, and observations.

Vocabulary
fuel

How do we use plants?

Plants are some of our most important natural resources. We use plants in many ways. Things like clothes and rugs come from cotton plants. Some plants are used to make medicine. The leaves of an aloe plant contain sap. This sap helps heal scrapes and burns. We use trees to make buildings, furniture, and paper.

log cabin

cotton

aloe

We also use some plants for food. What fruits and vegetables did you eat today? Foods like nuts, popcorn, and sugar all come from plants. The seeds of some plants are called grains. Grains can be ground into flour, which is used to make cereal and bread. We also feed grains to animals.

 What are some ways people use plants?

From Wheat to Bread

First the seeds inside the wheat are taken out. These seeds are called grains.

A mill grinds the wheat grains into flour.

The flour can be used to make bread. What else is made with flour?

Read a Diagram

Where does flour come from?

Science in Motion Play a game about resources @ **www.macmillanmh.com**

How do people use animals?

Animals are natural resources, too. Many people eat beef, chicken, fish, and other animals. We use milk from cows, goat, and sheep to make butter and cheese. Animals can be used for more than just food. Leather is made from the skins of animals. Some shoes and coats are made from leather. We also use animals for work. Farmers use animals to help them pull machines.

boots

milk

cheese

beef

▲ These things come from cows.

A **fuel** is something that gives off heat when it burns. We burn wood to give us heat. We also burn coal and oil. Long ago coal and oil formed underground from the remains of dead plants and animals. Now we use coal and oil to cook and heat our homes. Gasoline is a fuel made from oil.

▲ **Cars and trucks burn gasoline to move.**

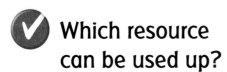 Which resource can be used up?

Think, Talk, and Write

1. **Summarize.** What are some ways people use plants?

2. Why is fuel important?

3. Write about an animal that people use for work.

Art Link

Make a poster to show how we use natural resources.

Be a Scientist

measuring cup

cream

jar

crackers

What happens when you shake cream?

Find out what will happen to cream when you shake it.

What to Do

1. **Measure.** Measure one quarter cup of cream.

2. Pour the cream into the jar. Put on the lid tightly.

Step 1

Step 2

3. Take turns shaking the jar.

2 IE 4.b. Measure length, weight, temperature, and liquid volume with appropriate tools and express those measurements in standard metric system units.

④ **Observe.** What happened to the cream? How did it change?

⑤ **Draw a Conclusion.** How do we use cream? Discuss your answers with a partner.

Investigate More

Communicate. How do people use chickens? What other animals are important to people? Why?

A World of Wool

Where does wool come from? Many people all over the world use sheep or goats to get wool. Some people get wool from other animals. Scientists at the American Museum of Natural History collect stories from people around the world. The scientists learn how people in other countries get wool.

Peru is a country in South America.

Dear Museum,

My name is Juana. I live in the Andes Mountains of Peru and the weather is cold. My family and I wear sweaters to keep us warm. Our sweaters are special because they are not made of sheep's wool. They are made of wool from llamas.

Llamas look like small camels. They have long necks and long legs. They have thick fur to keep them warm in the mountains. Some farmers in Peru raise llamas for their fur.

My wool sweater keeps me warm and dry in the winter!

Bye for now!

Juana

ELA R 2.2.5. Restate facts and details in the text to clarify and organize ideas.

▲ **People spin the llama's fur into yarn.**

Talk About It

Summarize. How do some people use llamas?

 **-Journal** Write about it online @ **www.macmillanmh.com**

AMERICAN MUSEUM ö NATURAL HISTORY

233
EXTEND

Resources of California

Look and Wonder

California is a sunny place.
How can we use light from the Sun?

Joshua Tree National Park, California

 2 ES 3.e. Students know rock, water, plants, and soil provide many resources, including food, fuel, and building materials, that humans use.

How can we use the Sun's light?

What to Do

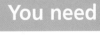

① Measure. Pour I cup of water into each bowl. Measure and record the temperatures.

Step ①

② Record Data. Put one bowl in a sunny place. Put the other in a dark place. Measure the temperatures at the end of the day.

③ Communicate. What happened to the water?

Explore More

④ Draw a Conclusion. How do we use the Sun's light?

You need

2 bowls

measuring cup

water

thermometer

 2 IE 4.b. Measure length, weight, temperature, and liquid volume with appropriate tools and express those measurements in standard metric system units.

Vocabulary

solar power

How does California get energy?

People in California use water, wind, and oil to make electric power. People also use light from the Sun. This is called **solar power**. Special machines called solar panels change sunlight into electric power. Some people put solar panels on their roofs to heat their homes.

Solar Power

Read a Photo

What do these solar panels use to make electric power?

In California, there is natural gas under the ground. Workers find this gas and store it in tanks. Some people burn natural gas for energy just like coal and oil. They can use natural gas to cook food and to heat their homes.

✔ How do people use solar power?

These people are cooking with natural gas.

▶ Some people drive cars that run on solar power!

What are other natural resources of California?

California is sunny and warm, and the soil is filled with minerals. The state is a great place to grow plants. Farmers in California can grow different kinds of crops, from avocados to walnuts. People all over the country eat fruits and vegetables from the Golden State.

Watsonville, California

▲ **Strawberries grow well in California.**

There are many other natural resources in California, too. People mine for gravel, clay, and silver. People also mine for gold. In the 1800s, many people rushed to California to find gold. Gold is still found in California today.

Gold miners from the 1800's.

 Why did people rush to California in the 1800s?

gold nugget

Think, Talk, and Write

1. **Summarize.** What are some natural resources of California?

2. What are some ways California gets electric power?

3. Write about why many fruits and vegetables grow well in California.

Health Link

Make a skit to tell your classmates why they should drink orange juice.

Sun Power

California is a warm sunny place. The Sun shines brightly in the sky. We get light and heat from the Sun.

Write About It

Why is California a good place to use solar power? Write a paragraph. Describe solar power and explain how people can use it.

Remember

When you explain, you write details.

LOG ON ⓔ-Journal Write about it online @ **www.macmillanmh.com**

ELA W 2.2.0. Students write compositions that describe and explain familiar objects, events, and experiences. Student writing demonstrates a command of standard American English and the drafting, research, and organizational strategies outlined in Writing Standard I.0.

Gold Rush

Suppose a miner went to California in 1849 to look for gold in the rivers. He looked for gold every day. Then one day, he found two nuggets of gold!

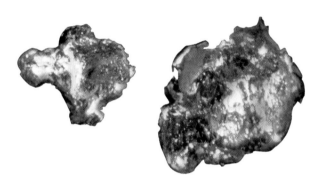

Figure It Out

The miner's first nugget was worth 75¢. His second nugget was worth twice as much as the first nugget.

How much money was the second nugget worth? How many quarters is that?

Remember
A quarter is worth 25¢.

MA NS 2.5.I. Solve problems using combinations of coins and bills.

Curious About Cotton

You know that we grow plants to give us food and wood. Did you know that we grow plants to give us clothes? Take a look at what you are wearing. What is made from plants? How do you know?

Cotton plants grow and make flowers. Then the flowers die and turn into green pods. These are the fruit. Each pod begins to grow bigger until it bursts open. When the cotton is ready to be picked, it looks like balls of white fluff.

What do you think cotton needs to grow? It needs a lot of sunshine, water, and good soil. Farmers in many parts of California grow cotton. People used to pick cotton by hand. Today machines pick the cotton.

The balls of cotton are full of leaves and seeds. Farmers take the balls to a machine that cleans the cotton. Then workers pack the cotton into huge piles called bales. They weigh about 500 pounds. That is as heavy as a horse!

The bales of cotton are sold to a mill. At the mill, the cotton is turned into thread. Then the thread is woven into cloth. The cloth is dyed different colors. Now it can be sewn into clothes for you to wear! What else is made from cotton?

Cotton can be used to make many things other than clothes. The paper for dollar bills is made from cotton. The oil from cottonseeds is used in foods like salad dressing. It is also used to make chairs! Farmers feed parts of the cotton plant to animals.

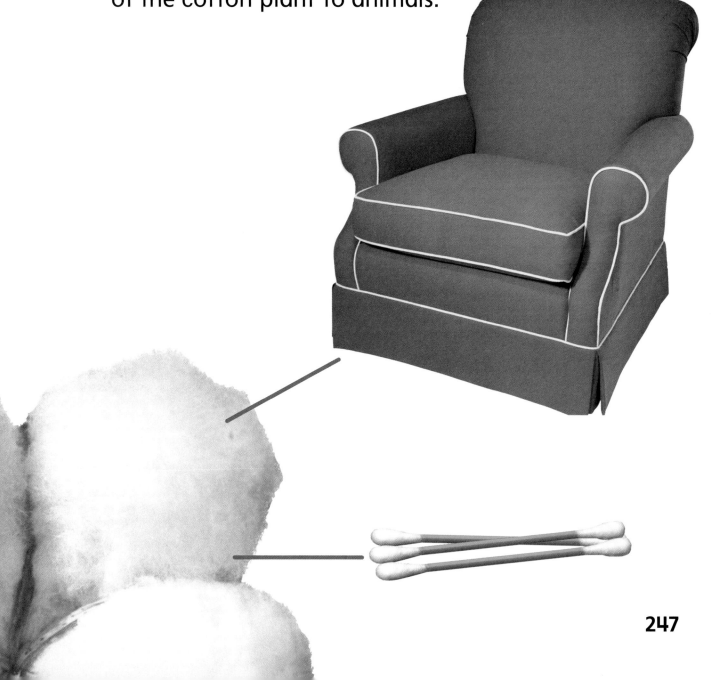

CHAPTER 5 Review

Vocabulary

fuel, page 229

natural resource, page 216

solar power, page 236

Use each word once for items 1-3.

1. Something that gives off heat when it is burned is called a _____. 2 ES 3.e

2. Plants are a _____. 2 ES 3.e

3. People can use sunlight to make electric power. This is called _____. 2 ES 3.e

4. Which of these things come from plants? Which come from animals? 2 ES 3.e

5. What are some natural resources? 2 ES 3.e

6. Discuss three items you use that come from natural resources. How do you use them? Where do they come from?

⭐ How do we use Earth's resources? 2 ES 3.e

CHAPTER 5

Eat Up!

Think about the last time you ate at a restaurant. What did you eat? Suppose you opened a restaurant. What would it look like? What would you serve?

▶ Make a menu for your restaurant. List five foods made from plants. List three foods made from animals.

▶ Describe your restaurant. What would the chairs and tables be made from? Will the napkins be made of cloth or paper?

▶ What other natural resources might you need for your restaurant?

2 ES 3.e. Students know rock, water, plants, and soil provide many resources, including food, fuel, and building materials, that humans use.

1 **The picture below shows a newspaper.**

What natural resource is it made from? 2 ES 3.e

A animals

B rocks

C trees

D soil

2 **Which of these comes from plants?** 2 ES 3.e

A glass of water

B cotton pants

C leather shoes

D a brick building

3 **What is a natural resource?** 2 ES 3.e

A something from nature that does not help people

B something that people make

C something from nature that helps people

D something from space that falls to Earth

Earthworms
Soil Helpers

All day long you are busy living on top of the Earth. At the same time, something is happening under your feet. Another kind of animal is busy working beneath the ground.

Earthworms live in the soil. They have no bones or legs. Yet they move up, down, and all around underground. Earthworms have no teeth, but they eat almost everything in their path.

2 ES 3.c. Students know that soil is made partly from weathered rock and partly from organic materials and that soils differ in their color, texture, capacity to retain water and ability to support the growth of many kinds of plants.
ELA R 2.2.0. Students read and understand grade-level appropriate material.

earthworm cocoon

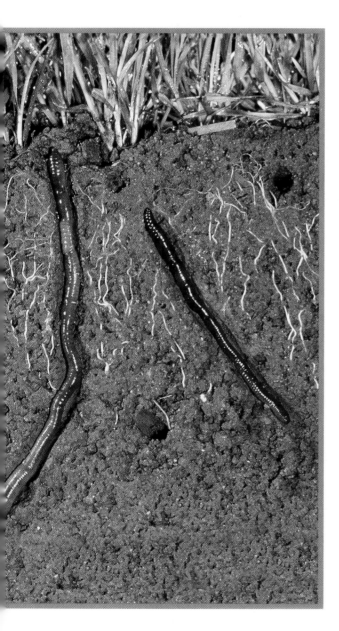

Earthworms do an important job. They swallow dirt and bits of dead plants and animals.

Then the worms leave castings behind. The castings help make rich new soil that is full of good food for plants.

Earthworms also make tunnels and mix the soil. This helps the roots of plants grow and spread. Worms are nature's soil helpers!

seeding in soil

Careers in Science

Paleontologist

Do you like to learn about dinosaurs? Someday you could be a paleontologist. A paleontologist learns about animals and plants that lived on Earth long ago. These scientists dig in the ground to look for fossils. They study the fossils to find out more about what life was like in the past.

Paleontologists find more than just dinosaur fossils. These scientists have found fossils of fish, plants, and insects. They have even found fossils of worm tracks.

paleontologist

More Careers to Think About

fossil reconstructor

model maker

LOG ON e-Careers @ www.macmillanmh.com

Physical Science

George W. Ferris designed the first Ferris wheel in 1893.

Objects in Motion

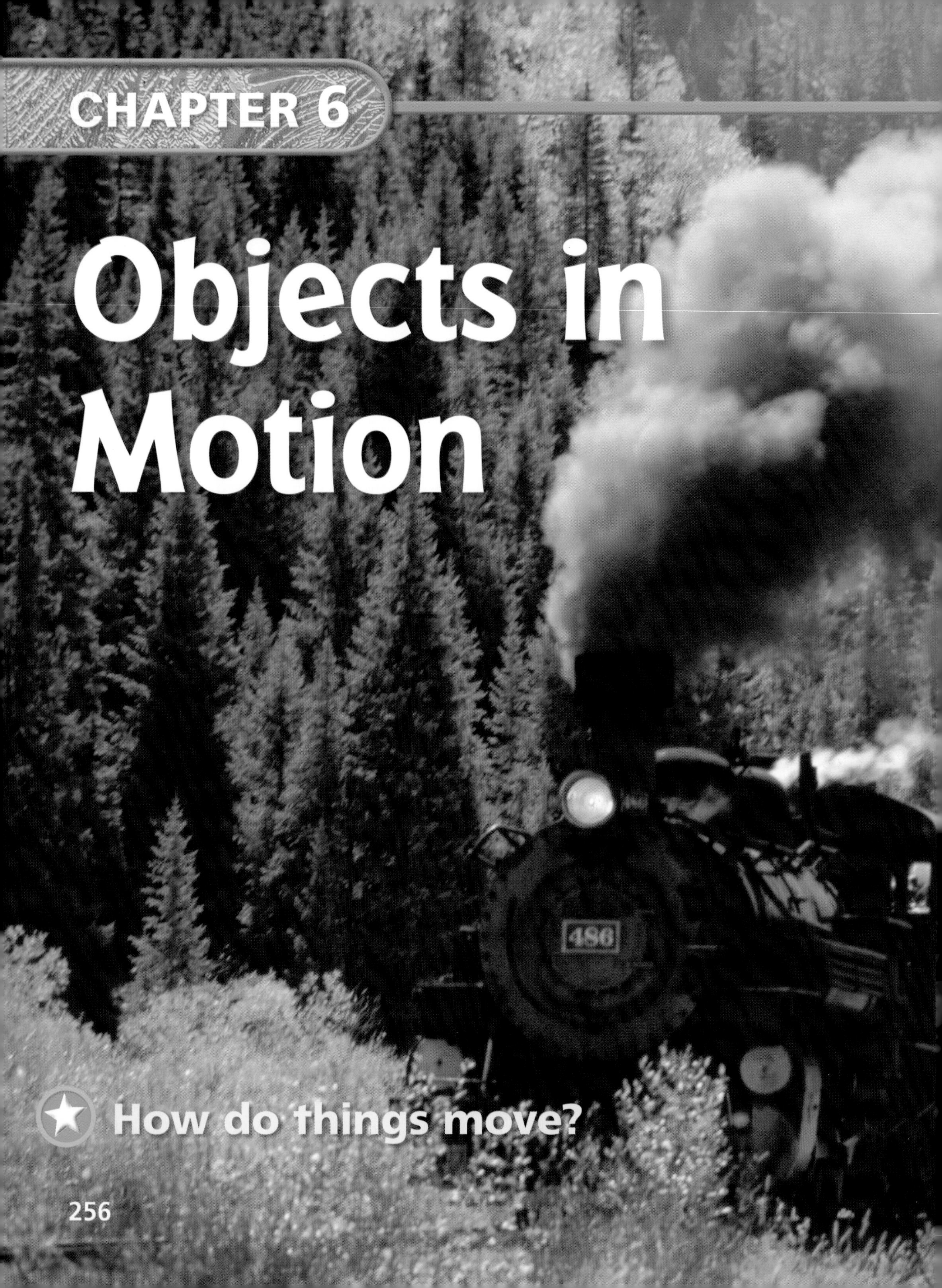

★ How do things move?

 2 PS I. The motion of objects can be observed and measured.

257

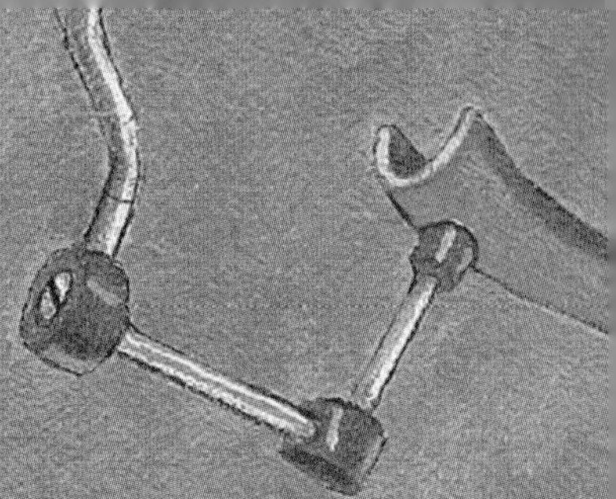

Literature
Poem

ELA R 2.2.0. Students read and understand grade-level appropriate material.

If

by James Stevenson

If you knew what to turn,

If you knew what to twist,

If you knew what to push and pull

   And snap and click

   And crank and yank,

Then this machine would probably do

Whatever it is

It's suppposed to do.

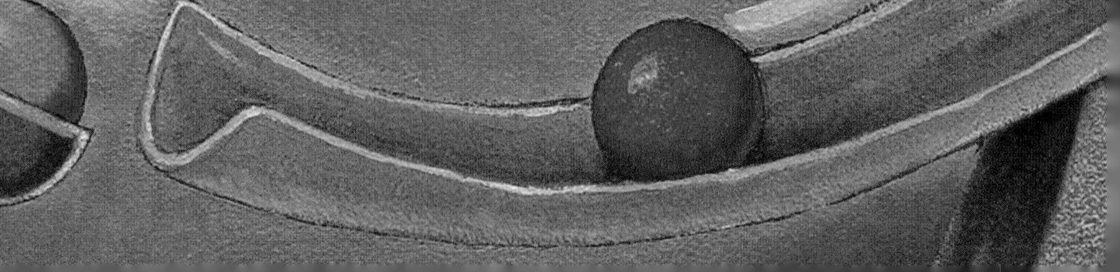

Talk About It

What do you think this machine could do?

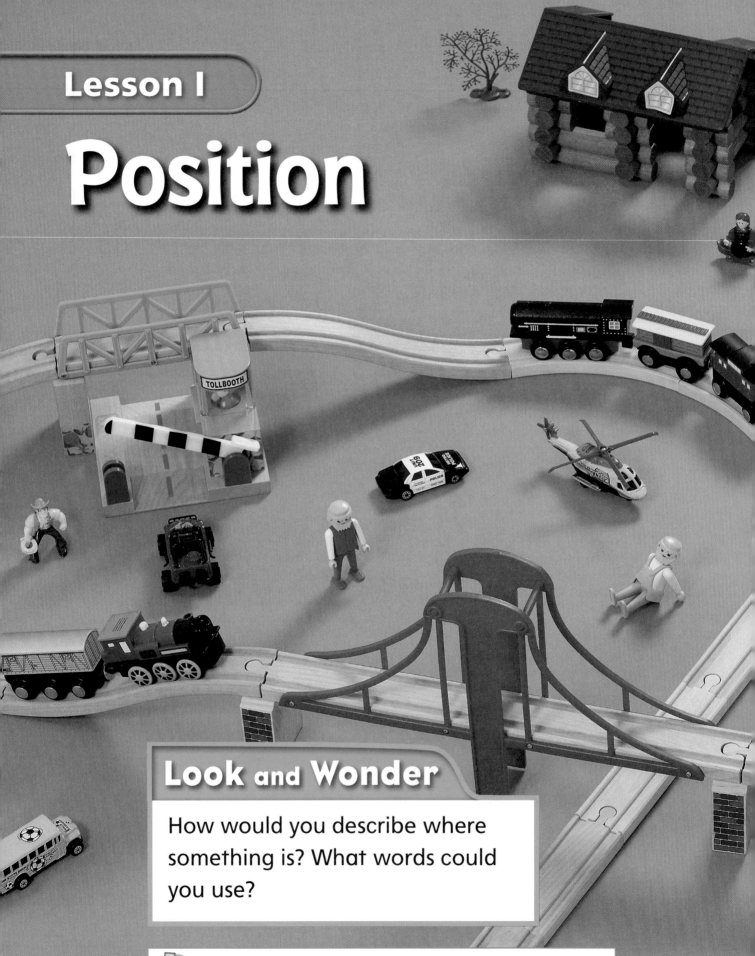

Position

Look and Wonder

How would you describe where something is? What words could you use?

2 PS 1.a. Students know the position of an object can be described by locating it in relation to another object or to the background.

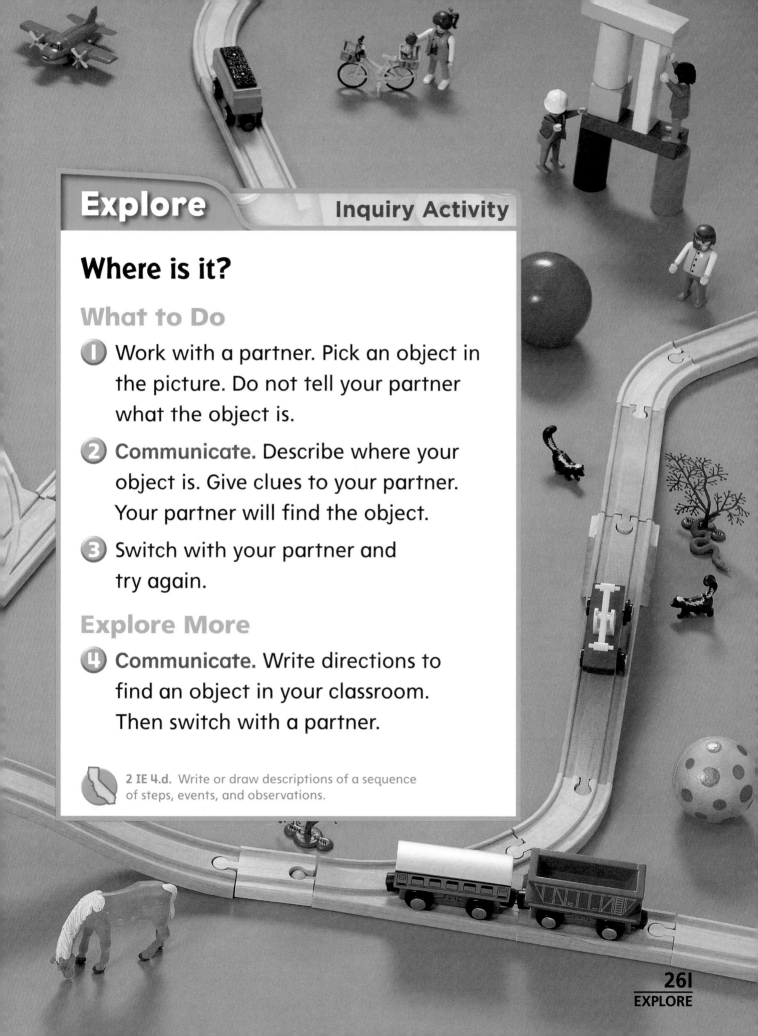

Explore

Where is it?

What to Do

1. Work with a partner. Pick an object in the picture. Do not tell your partner what the object is.

2. **Communicate.** Describe where your object is. Give clues to your partner. Your partner will find the object.

3. Switch with your partner and try again.

Explore More

4. **Communicate.** Write directions to find an object in your classroom. Then switch with a partner.

2 IE 4.d. Write or draw descriptions of a sequence of steps, events, and observations.

Vocabulary

position

distance

How can you describe where something is?

Position is the place where something is. You can tell the position of an object by comparing it to something that does not move. You can use words such as above, below, left, right, near, far, next to, in, on, and under to describe position. What other words describe position?

▲ **The orange fish is to the left of the chest.**

When something moves, its position changes. You can describe its new position by comparing it to other objects.

 How do you tell the position of an object?

▲ **Where is the orange fish now? How did it move?**

How do you measure distance?

Look around you. What is close to you? Your desk is close to you. The board is near where you sit.

What is far from you? The playground is far from where you sit. Washington, DC, is very far away from you. **Distance** is how far away one thing is from another. One way you can measure distance is by using a map.

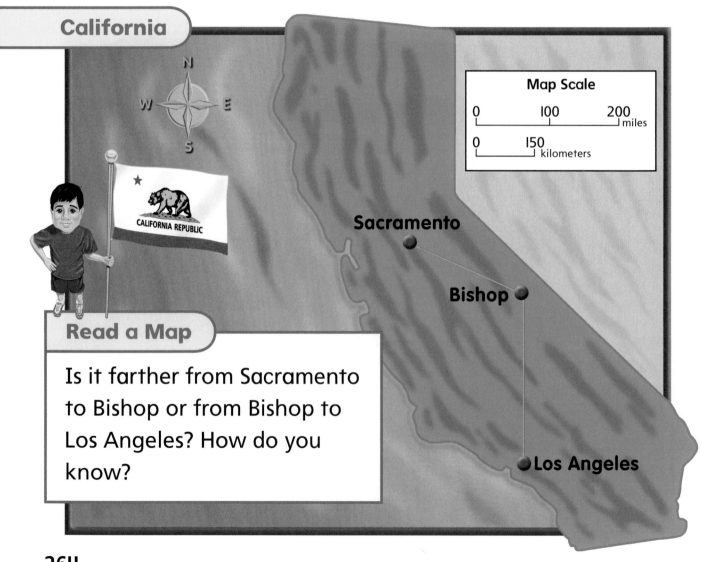

California

Map Scale

0   100   200
                          miles

0   150
              kilometers

Sacramento

Bishop

Los Angeles

Read a Map

Is it farther from Sacramento to Bishop or from Bishop to Los Angeles? How do you know?

You can use units such as inches, feet, and miles to measure distance. You can also use metric units such as centimeters, meters, and kilometers.

 What is the distance from the frog to the fly?

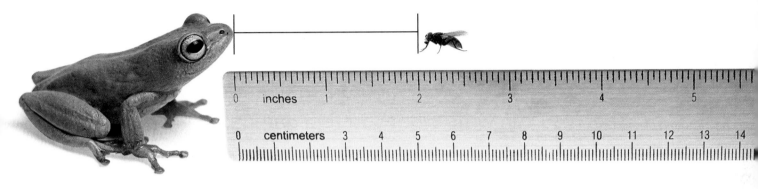

Think, Talk, and Write

1. **Cause and Effect.** Two friends stand next to each other. How can you make the distance between them greater?

2. What are some words that describe position?

3. Write about a place that is far from you.

Math Link

Measure an object in inches and centimeters. Which is bigger, 1 inch or 1 centimeter?

Focus on Skills

Measure

When you **measure** distance, you find out how far two objects are from one another.

Learn It

Measure the distance between your elbow and your fingertips. You can measure in inches or centimeters. You can even measure in paper clips! Then you can write what you find out in a chart.

Distance from Elbow to Fingertips			
	inches	centimeters	paper clips
Jamal	9	22	7
Sarah	8	20	6

2 IE 4.b. Measure length, weight, temperature, and liquid volume with appropriate tools and express those measurements in standard metric system units.

Try It

Make a starting line on the floor. Jump! Put tape where your feet land. Use a ruler to measure how far you jumped. Use centimeters and inches. Then line up paper clips to measure how far you jumped. Record what you find out on a chart.

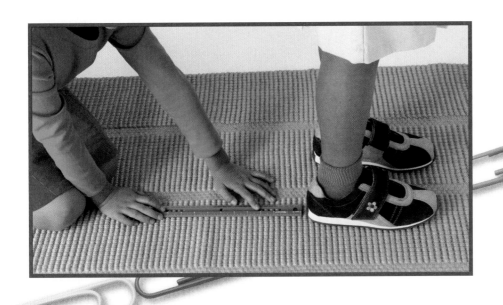

I. How many inches was the longest jump?

2. How many paper clips was the shortest jump?

3. Write About It. What else can you use to measure distance?

Motion

Look and Wonder

How would you describe
the motion of this roller coaster?

2 PS I.b. Students know an object's motion can be described by recording the change in position of the object over time.

Inquiry Activity

How do different things move?

What to Do

① Work with a partner. Put two small objects on a table. Tap each object.

② **Observe.** How did each object move?

Explore More

③ **Predict.** Try moving other objects. Which object do you think will travel the farthest? Why do you think so?

You need

small objects

Step ①

 2 IE 4.a. Make predictions based on observed patterns and not random guessing.

Vocabulary

motion

speed

SCIENCE QUEST Explore motion with the Treasure Hunters.

How can you tell if something has moved?

All around you, things move. People walk up and down the street. Leaves fall off a tree and blow in the wind. When something moves, it starts from one position. Then it ends in another position. You can see how the position changed.

When something is moving, we say it is in **motion**. Motion is a change in position. This diver is in motion. She starts at the top of a diving board. She jumps into the air and dives into the pool. Her position changed.

 Describe a motion you do every day. How does your position change?

What is speed?

Have you ever watched a race? Most people can run half a mile in 5 minutes. An Olympic runner can run 1 mile in just 5 minutes or less! **Speed** is how far something moves in a certain amount of time.

Animal Speeds

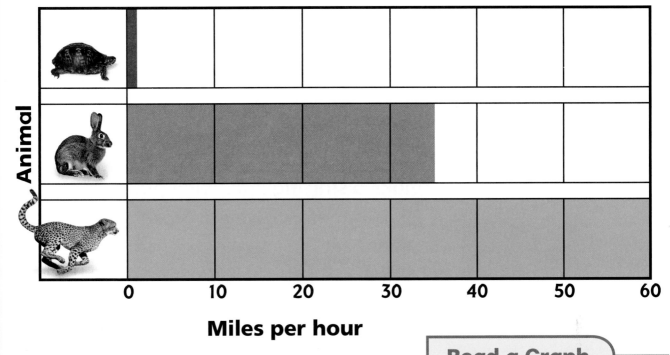

Animal

Miles per hour

0   10   20   30   40   50   60

Read a Graph

Which is the fastest animal?

 How fast would you have to go to beat a cheetah in a race?

Think, Talk, and Write

1. **Cause and Effect.** A girl is walking to school. How can she get there faster?

2. How do you know if something is in motion?

3. Write about something that moves slowly.

Art Link

Draw a picture of something that moves quickly.

Be a Scientist

You need

masking tape

ruler

windup toys

stopwatch

Which toy moves faster?

You can compare the speeds of objects.

What to Do

1. **Measure.** Put tape on the floor to make a starting line. Then put tape 20 centimeters away to make a finish line.

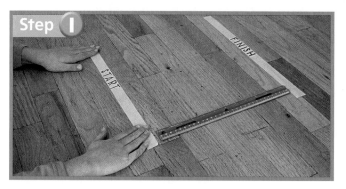

Step 1

2. Wind up a toy. When you let go of the toy at the starting line, have your partner start the stopwatch. When the toy crosses the finish line, stop the watch. Record how long it took for the toy to finish.

Step 2

2 IE 4.a. Make predictions based on observed patterns and not random guessing.

3 Wind up another toy and repeat the steps.

4 **Compare.** Which toy was faster? If you did not have a stopwatch to measure the time, how could you find out which toy was faster?

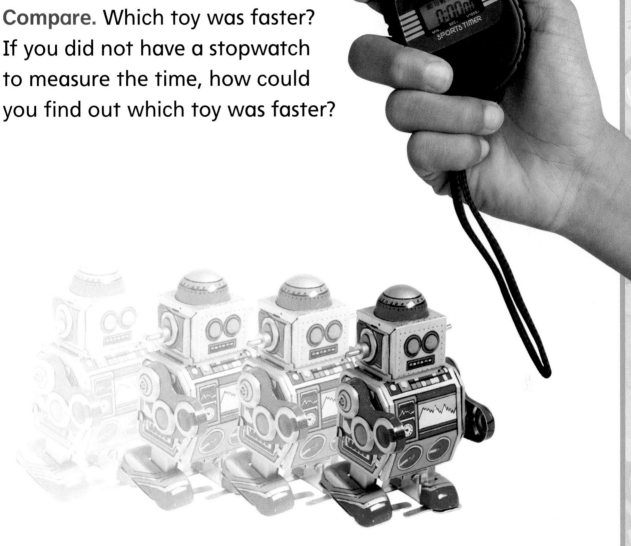

Investigate More

If the finish line were farther away, would the same toy win? How could you check your answer?

Pushes and Pulls

Look and Wonder

How can you make something move?
How can you make it move farther?

2 PS I.c. Students know the way to change how something is moving is by giving it a push or pull. The size of the change is related to the strength, or the amount of force, of the push or pull.

How do you make things go farther and faster?

You need

toy car

masking tape

ruler

What to Do

① Line up the car at a starting line. Push the car gently over the line.

Step ①

START

② **Measure.** How far did it go?

③ Do the activity again, but this time push the car harder. Observe what happens.

Explore More

④ **Predict.** What do you think would happen if you pulled the car toward you? Would it go as far?

Step ②

START

 2 IE 4.b. Measure length, weight, temperature, and liquid volume with appropriate tools and express those measurements in standard metric system units.

Vocabulary

force

push

pull

What are forces?

Things can not move on their own. You have to use a **force** to put something in motion. When you play soccer, you kick the ball to move it across the field. Your kick is a force. If you do not kick the ball, it will stay in the same place. Soccer would be very boring without forces!

Kicking

Read a Photo

How can this girl make the ball move farther?

A push or a pull is called a force. If you **push** something, it will move away from you. If you **pull** it, it will move closer to you. A kick is a kind of push. When you open a drawer, you pull it toward yourself. What things do you push and pull every day?

 Why do we need forces?

▼ **In this game, the children on each side of the rope pull.**

What happens when a force changes?

You know that when you use a lot of force to throw a ball, it goes far. If you toss the ball lightly, it will not go as far. When you use more force, things move faster and go farther. When you use less force, things move slower and do not go as far.

Have you ever moved something heavy? Was it easy to move? You know that light things are easier to move than heavier things. You have to use more force to move something heavy. Some objects are so heavy that people use handcarts, trucks, or cranes to move them.

 How can you move something heavy?

▼ **Do you think this boy is using a lot of force or a little? How do you know?**

Think, Talk, and Write

1. **Cause and Effect.** What happens when you pull something harder?

2. Which is harder to move, a pencil or a brick? Why?

3. Write about how you use pushes and pulls every day.

Health Link

Push and pull to exercise your muscles.

Travel Through Time

People have always liked to travel. They found ways to travel across the state, across the country, and across the world. Now people have even traveled to space! The time line below shows the first machines that helped people travel to far places.

1804

In England, Richard Trevithick built the first steam engine for a train. The steam engine helped people travel over long distances. It also helped them get to places faster.

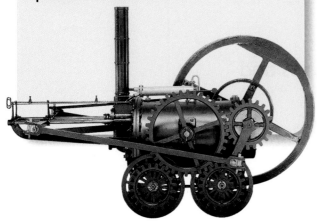

1884

In Germany, Karl Friedrich Benz built the first car to run on gas. It worked like the cars you see today. His car had only three wheels!

 ELA R 2.2.7. Interpret information from diagrams, charts, and graphs.

1903

Wilbur and Orville Wright built the first airplane that flew and landed safely. Their plane had an engine that ran on gas. It flew over 120 feet for 12 seconds.

1961

Russian astronaut Yuri Gagarin was the first person in space. His spaceship had special engines that were stronger than the force of Earth's gravity. The engines helped the spaceship leave Earth.

Talk About It

Sequence. How have cars changed over time?

LOG ON e-Journal Write about it online @ www.macmillanmh.com

AMERICAN MUSEUM OF NATURAL HISTORY

Changing Motion

Look and Wonder

Why do you think this girl can slide?

 2 PS I.c. Students know the way to change how something is moving is by giving it a push or pull. The size of the change is related to the strength, or the amount of force, of the push or pull.

How can you slow something down?

You need

cardboard

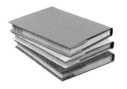

books

toy car

ruler

sandpaper

What to Do

1 Make a ramp out of books and cardboard.

Step 1

2 **Measure.** Put the car at the top of the ramp and let go. Do not push it. Measure how far the car went.

3 **Compare.** Tape sandpaper to the cardboard. Repeat the activity. Which ramp slowed the car down more?

Explore More

4 **Predict.** What would happen if you put cloth on the ramp?

2 IE 4.b. Measure length, weight, temperature, and liquid volume with appropriate tools and express those measurements in standard metric system units.

Vocabulary

friction

What slows things down?

Friction is a force that slows down moving things. Friction happens when two things rub together. There is more friction on rough surfaces than on smooth ones. It is harder to push or pull something on a rough surface than on a smooth surface.

▲ The thick treads on tires help cars drive over slippery roads. The treads add friction between the car and the road.

▲ To slow down when you skate, you drag a rubber stopper on the ground. The dragging causes friction.

Sometimes friction is helpful. Running shoes have treads that add friction. The shoes keep runners from slipping and falling. Other times we try to have less friction to make things easier to move. The bottoms of ballet slippers are smooth so dancers can slide across the floor easily.

 How can friction help us?

◀ The bottoms of surfboards are smooth so that surfers can glide on the waves.

How can forces change motion?

You know that forces can change the motion of things. Forces can make things speed up, slow down, stop, and start moving. They can make things change direction, too. In a game of softball, the players use force to change the direction of a ball's motion.

 Think of a sport that uses a ball. How does the ball change direction?

How a Ball Changes Direction

▲ The pitcher uses force to throw the ball toward the batter.

◄ The batter uses a push to hit the ball. It changes direction and flies toward the outfield.

▶ The player in the field catches the ball and stops its motion. He can use a force to throw the ball to another player.

Read a Diagram

What kind of force do the players use?

LOG ON *Science in Motion* Watch forces at work @ **www.macmillanmh.com**

Think, Talk, and Write

1. **Cause and Effect.** What causes friction?

2. Why is it hard to push something on a rough surface?

3. Write about a time you played with a ball. How did the ball change direction?

Social Studies Link

Learn about a sport played in another country. Describe the pushes and pulls in this sport.

Slip and Slide

Have you ever walked on ice? It is smooth and slippery! Sometimes penguins slide on their bellies to move.

 ## Write About It

Explain why penguins can slide on the ice. Make sure to explain why ice is slippery.

Remember

When you write to give information, you give facts.

 -Journal Write about it online @ **www.macmillanmh.com**

 ELA W 2.2.0 Students write compositions that describe and explain familiar objects, events, and experiences. Student writing demonstrates a command of standard American English and the drafting, research, and organizational strategies outlined in Writing Standard I.0.

How far did it move?

These students are playing softball.
They want to know how far the ball moved.

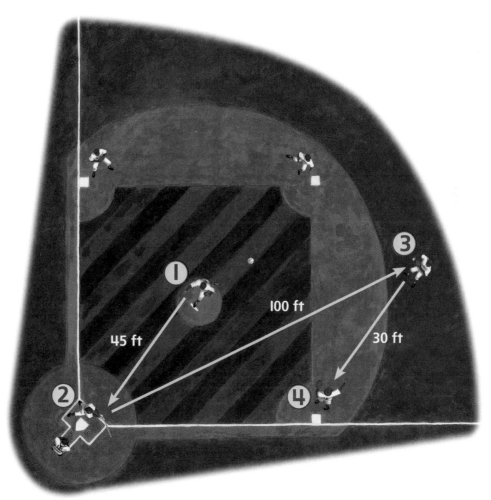

100 ft

45 ft

30 ft

① ② ③ ④

Add Measurements

Add the distances the ball moved.
How far did it go? How many times
did the ball change directions? Now
make up your own math problem
about the softball game.

Remember
Add the 1s first.
Then add the
10s. Then add
the 100s.

MA NS 2.2.2. Find the sum or difference of two whole numbers
up to three digits long.

Roller Coaster Ride

We get on and sit side by side.

The bar snaps us into our seats.

Once we are in place, we begin the ride!

We start with a jerk and move away.

Slowly we begin to climb.

We have been waiting for this all day!

We move up and up to the top of the hill

It will not be long until our biggest thrill!

293

We go over the top and here we go!

Down and around we fly, faster and faster.

Then up and around and down again,

We yell and scream into the wind!

As we go up the hill, we lose some speed.

Soon we zoom down and get
the speed we need to make it
to the top of the next hill.

Above the trees, we are up so high,

Next to the birds in the sky!

We are upside down! AAAHHH!

We loop around,

We look all the way down
to the ground!

I scream and shut my eyes!

Around another turn we go.

I want to get off!

When will this coaster stop?

Then screeeeeech!

We come to the end!

Now that we are safely back on the ground.

I can not wait to go again!

Vocabulary

friction, page 286

position, page 262

pull, page 279

push, page 279

speed, page 272

Use each word once for items 1–7.

1. When you tell where something is, you describe its _____. 2 PS I.a

2. When you tell how fast something moves in a certain amount of time, you tell its _____. 2 PS I.b

3. A force that slows down moving things is _____. 2 PS I.c

4. This picture shows a force called a _____. 2 PS I.c

5. This picture shows a force called a _____. 2 PS I.c

6. **Communicate.** Describe the position of the cat in as many ways as you can. 2 PS I.a

7. When would you want more friction? When would you want less? 2 PS I.c

8. **Cause and Effect.** What force do basketball players use when they make a basket? 2 PS I.c

⭐ How do things move? 2 PS I.b

CHAPTER 6

Pushes and Pulls

You use pushes and pulls every day. Use the pictures to answer the questions below.

▶ Write a sentence about each picture. What force is used?

▶ How would the pictures change if the people used more or less force?

▶ Look at the pictures. Which activity do you need the most force to do? How do you know?

1 **What happens when you pull something?** 2 PS I.c

   A It moves toward you.

   B It moves in a circle.

   C It moves away from you.

   D It floats away.

2 **Rosa walked to school on Monday. It took her 10 minutes. On Tuesday she walked the same way but it took her 15 minutes. What changed?** 2 PS I.b

   A her speed

   B the amount of friction

   C the distance

   D her direction

3 **Look at the picture below.**

What is the position of the painting in this diagram? 2 PS I.a

   A The painting is under the sofa.

   B The painting is to the left of the sofa.

   C The painting is in front of the sofa.

   D The painting is above the sofa.

Forces at Work

⭐ What can forces do?

 2 PS 1. The motion of objects can be observed and measured.

303

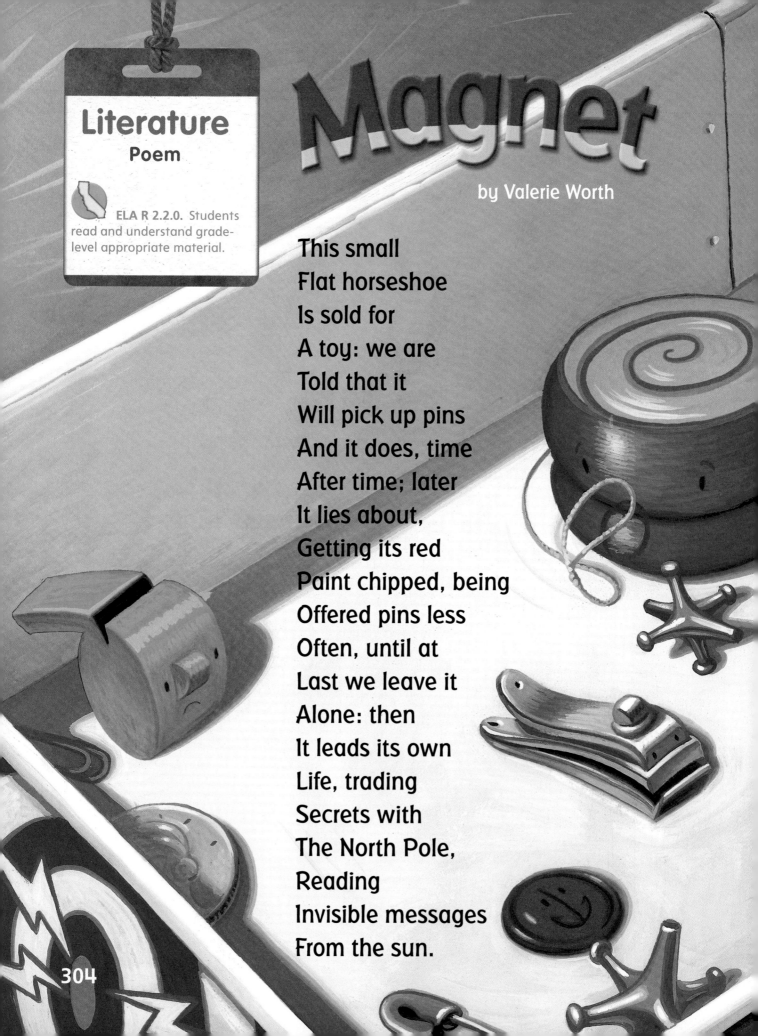

Literature
Poem

ELA R 2.2.0. Students read and understand grade-level appropriate material.

Magnet

by Valerie Worth

This small
Flat horseshoe
Is sold for
A toy: we are
Told that it
Will pick up pins
And it does, time
After time; later
It lies about,
Getting its red
Paint chipped, being
Offered pins less
Often, until at
Last we leave it
Alone: then
It leads its own
Life, trading
Secrets with
The North Pole,
Reading
Invisible messages
From the sun.

Talk About It

What can you do with a magnet?

305

Tools and Machines

Look and Wonder

How can the woman lift this car?

 2 PS I.d. Students know tools and machines are used to apply pushes and pulls (forces) to make things move.

How can a push help you lift something?

What to Do

1 Tape a pencil to your desk.

2 Put the second pencil across the first pencil.

3 Put a book on one side of the second pencil. Then lift the book by pushing the pencil down.

Step **3**

You need

tape

2 pencils

book

goggles

Explore More

4 **Predict.** What would happen if you moved the book closer to the taped pencil? Try it.

 2 IE 4.a. Make predictions based on observed patterns and not random guessing.

Vocabulary

simple machine

lever

ramp

tool

What makes work easier?

A **simple machine** can make moving an object easier. It makes the force of your push or pull stronger. When you lifted a book using two pencils, you used a simple machine. This type of simple machine is called a **lever**. A lever lets you use less force to move something. You use levers all the time. Some examples of levers are seesaws, forks, and scissors.

▼ You can use a lever to open a can of paint. First you put a metal stick under the lid. Then you press down on the stick. The lid will lift up.

A **ramp** is also a simple machine. Ramps can help you move things to a higher place. It is easier to push something up a ramp than to lift it up. Another simple machine that helps you move things is a wheel. Wheels let people roll objects instead of lift them.

▲ **Pushing the box up a ramp is easier than lifting it up.**

 What levers and wheels do you use every day?

▼ **The wheels on the stroller make it easier for the girl to push her brother.**

What is a tool?

A **tool** can be a simple machine or it can be made up of many simple machines. A hammer is a tool made of one simple machine. It is a lever that can be used to pry nails loose. An engine is made up of many simple machines. All the parts work together to make a car move.

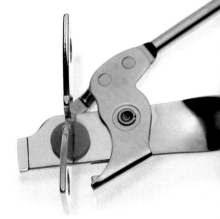

can opener

 How does an engine make work easier?

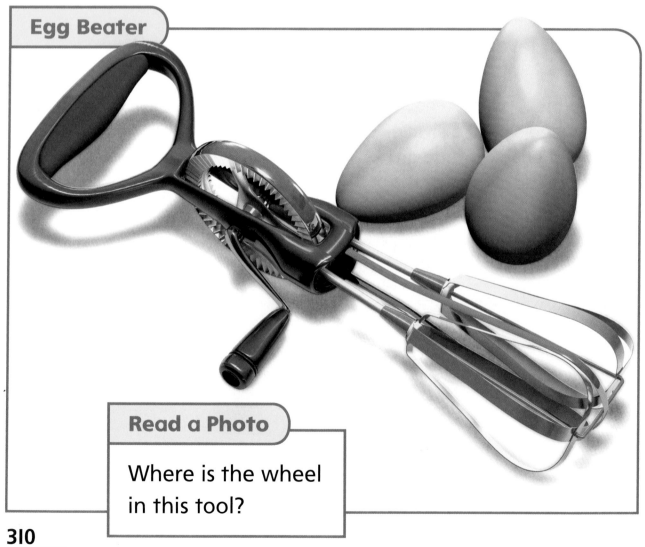

Egg Beater

Read a Photo

Where is the wheel in this tool?

What simple machines are in these three tools?

spatula

nutcracker

Think, Talk, and Write

1. **Predict.** How many bricks could you lift with your arms? How many could you lift with a lever?

2. Describe some tools and machines.

3. **Write About It.** What tools and machines did you use today? How did they help you?

Math Link

Make a chart of simple machines you see in your classroom.

Predict

When you **predict**, you describe what you think will happen. You use information about what has happened before to decide what could happen next.

Learn It

Joe and Larissa need to move boxes up to their apartments. Who do you think will finish first?

Larissa   Joe

What I Know

I Know it takes longer to climb stairs than to take an elevator.

➡️

What I Predict

I predict that Larissa will finish last.

 2 IE 4.a. Make predictions based on observed patterns and not random guessing.

Try It

Miguel and Eric have a race.
Miguel runs and Eric roller skates.

1. **Predict.** Who do you think will win? Why?

2. What information did you use
   to help you predict?

3. **Write About It.** Write a story about a race
   that uses simple machines.

Gravity

Look and Wonder

What do you think will happen to the dog and the ball?

 2 PS I.e. Students know objects fall to the ground unless something holds them up.

Does one fall faster?

What to Do

1. Put the newspaper on the floor.

2. Let go of the two lemons at exactly the same time.

3. Have a partner watch to see which one hits the ground first.

4. **Predict.** What will happen if you let go of a grape and a lemon at the same time?

Explore More

5. Try this activity with an object that is heavier than a lemon. Which one falls first?

 2 IE 4.a. Make predictions based on observed patterns and not random guessing.

You need

newspaper

2 lemons

1 grape

Step **2**

Vocabulary

gravity

weight

What is gravity?

Gravity is a force that pulls things toward each other. All things have a force of gravity. The larger an object is, the stronger the force of gravity it has. Even though you can not see gravity, you can feel it. Gravity is what keeps you on the ground. It pulls you back to the ground when you jump in the air. Without gravity, you would fly into outer space.

Gravity at Work

Read a Diagram

Which has a stronger force of gravity, the ball or Earth?

LOG ON *Science in Motion* Watch this diagram in action @ **www.macmillanmh.com**

Earth has a strong force of gravity because of its size. The gravity of Earth is stronger than the gravity of smaller things. That is why a ball in the air will fall back down to Earth.

 Why do things fall down to Earth?

What is weight?

Gravity pulls everything toward the center of Earth with a certain amount of force. This amount of force is called **weight**. You can find the weight of an object by putting it on a scale. A scale is a tool used to measure the amount of gravity that pulls on objects. A scale can measure in ounces, pounds, or even tons.

The guinea pig weighs about 2 pounds.
The pumpkin weighs about 7 pounds.

Planets and moons have more or less gravity than Earth. Our Moon is much smaller than Earth. This means that it has less gravity than Earth. Things will weigh less on the Moon than on Earth. If you weighed 60 pounds on Earth, you would weigh about 10 pounds on the Moon!

 Would the pumpkin weigh more or less on the Moon?

▲ The astronaut can jump high on the Moon because there is less gravity that pulls him down.

Think, Talk, and Write

1. What force keeps you on the ground?

2. What is weight?

3. How do you think it would feel to walk in outer space? Write a paragraph.

Health Link

Learn about what foods astronauts eat in space to stay healthy.

Meet Hector Arce

Gravity is the force that keeps you on Earth. You may not be able to see gravity, but it is all around you. In fact, it is everywhere! There is gravity on planets, moons, and stars. How powerful is gravity? It is powerful enough to create a star!

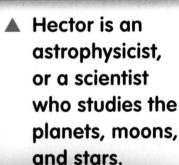

▲ Hector is an astrophysicist, or a scientist who studies the planets, moons, and stars.

ELA R 2.2.6. Recognize cause-and-effect relationships in a text.

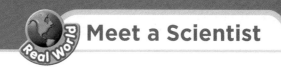
Hector Arce is a scientist at the American Museum of Natural History. Hector studies how stars form. When gravity pulls together huge clouds of gas and dust, stars form. Gravity makes their centers so hot that they light up. This is why stars shine in our night sky.

Talk About It

Cause and Effect.

How do stars form?

LOG ON e-Journal Write about it online @ **www.macmillanmh.com**

▼ **Hector uses a telescope like the one in this building to get a closer look at stars.**

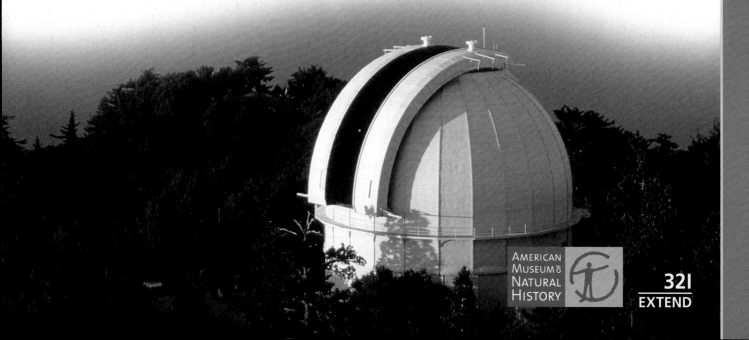

AMERICAN
MUSEUM OF
NATURAL
HISTORY

Magnets Push, Magnets Pull

Look and Wonder

Why does the magnet pull some of these objects and not others?

2 PS I.f. Students know magnets can be used to make some objects move without being touched.

What sticks to a magnet?

What to Do

1. Tie string to a pencil. Tie a magnet to the end of the string.

Step 1

2. **Predict.** Put the objects in a bag. Which objects will stick to the magnet?

3. Use the magnet to pull out objects from the bag.

Explore More

4. **Classify.** How are the things that stick to the magnet alike?

2 IE 4.c. Compare and sort common objects according to two or more physical attributes (e.g., color, shape, texture, size, weight).

You need

string

pencil

magnet

small objects

paper bag

Read Together and Learn

Vocabulary
attract
poles
repel

What does a magnet pull?

A magnet can push and pull. This is called magnetic force. A magnet can **attract**, or pull, objects made of iron. A magnet will not attract a penny because it is not made of iron. Is a quarter made of iron? How could you find out?

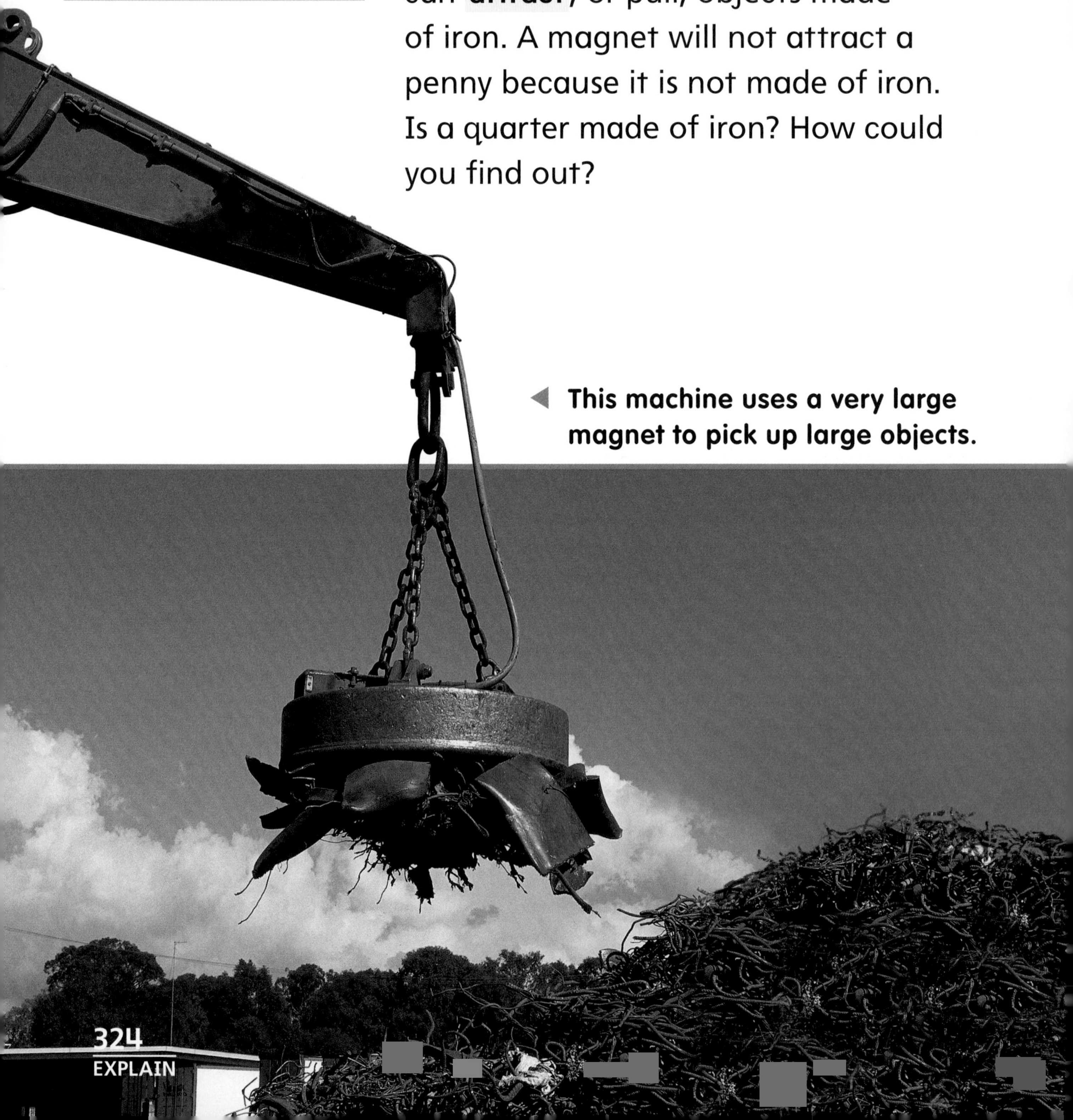

This machine uses a very large magnet to pick up large objects.

Magnets can move things without even touching them. Magnets can pull through solids like paper, plastic, or glass. They can pull through liquids and gases, too. Every magnet has a magnetic field. This is the area around a magnet where its force pulls.

brass pot

aluminum can

gold ring

▲ A magnet will not attract objects made of brass, gold, or aluminum.

▶ Magnets can pull through liquids and solids.

✔ Will a magnet attract a rubber band? Why or why not?

What are poles?

Magnets have two **poles**, a north pole and a south pole. The poles are where the pull of the magnet is strongest. A magnet's pull is stronger on iron objects that are close than on objects that are farther away.

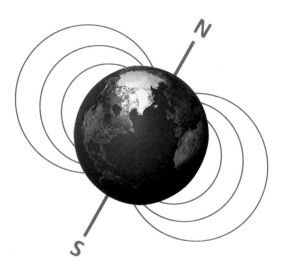

▲ The Earth has a magnetic field. It has two poles, a north pole and a south pole.

Magnet

N   S

Read a Photo

Where does this magnet attract the most iron?

The poles of these magnets attract each other because they are opposites. A north pole and a south pole pull toward each other.

attract

The poles of these magnets **repel**, or push away from each other. They repel each other because they are the same.

repel

✔ Which poles attract each other?

Think, Talk, and Write

1. **Predict.** What will happen when you put foil near a magnet? Try it.

2. When will two magnets repel each other?

3. Write about how you could use magnets.

Art Link

Make a sculpture using magnets and objects.

Be a Scientist

paper clips

magnets

How can you compare the strengths of different magnets?

Find out how many paper clips the magnets can attract.

What to Do

① Hang a paper clip from a magnet. Keep adding more clips in a line until no more will stick.

Step **①**

 2 IE 4.e. Construct bar graphs to record data, using appropriately labeled axes.

2 **Record Data.** Write how many paper clips can hang from the magnet.

3 **Repeat** the steps using different magnets.

4 **Communicate.** Make a bar graph to show the strengths of your magnets.

Investigate More

Communicate. Stick two magnets together. How many paper clips can hang from them? Why do you think this happens?

Sound

Look and Wonder

How are these people making sound?

 2 PS I.g. Students know sound is made by vibrating objects and can be described by its pitch and volume.

How is sound made?

What to Do

You need

string

paper clip

paper cup

① Work with two partners. Tie string to a paper clip. Make a hole in the cup. Pull the string through the hole.

Step ①

② Hold the cup and string with one partner. The third partner snaps the string.

③ **Observe.** What happened to the string? How did you make sound?

Explore More

④ **Predict.** Change the length of the string. Predict what will happen. How does the sound change?

 2 IE 4.d. Write or draw descriptions of a sequence of steps, events, and observations.

Step ②

Vocabulary

sound

vibrates

volume

pitch

 **SCIENCE QUEST** Explore sound with the Treasure Hunters.

What is sound?

Sound is a kind of energy you hear. Sound is made when something **vibrates**, or moves back and forth. When you snap a string, it vibrates. The air around it vibrates, too. The vibrating air goes to your ear. A part of your ear called the eardrum vibrates, and then you hear the sound.

How We Hear Sound

▼ When a person plucks a guitar string, it vibrates.

▼ The vibrating air travels to your ear.

▼ When your eardrum vibrates, you hear the sound!

Read a Diagram

Which part of your ear vibrates?

When you speak, air moves from your lungs to your throat. The air moves over your vocal cords and causes the vocal cords to vibrate. Touch your throat as you speak. What do you feel?

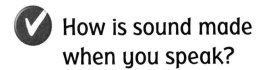 How is sound made when you speak?

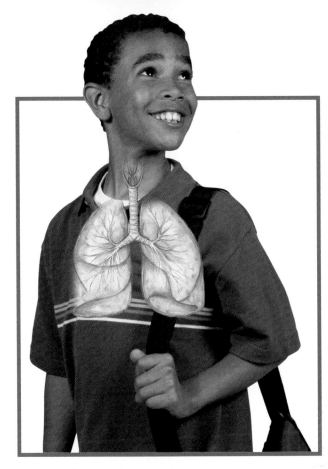

▲ When you speak, your vocal cords vibrate.

▶ When you blow air through a flute, it vibrates and makes a sound.

What makes sounds loud or soft?

When a sound is loud, the vibrations are big. When a sound is soft, the vibrations are small. When you yell, you make big vibrations in your throat. When you whisper, you make smaller vibrations. **Volume** describes the loudness of a sound.

cat's meow

▲ A lion's roar can be so loud that you can hear it up to 6 miles away!

Think about a lion's roar. When you are near the lion, the roar sounds loud. When you are far away, the roar sounds soft. The farther away you are from a sound, the softer it sounds to you. Most animals can hear soft sounds that people can not hear. These animals use their hearing to hunt and communicate with each other.

 What happens when you move far away from a sound?

What is pitch?

Sounds can be high, low, or in between. **Pitch** describes how high or low a sound is. When a sound is low, the vibrations are slow. Some sounds with low pitch are a cow's moo and a man's voice.

◀ When you hit a small bar, the pitch is high. When you hit a big bar, the pitch is low.

high pitch

low pitch

When a sound has a high pitch, the vibrations are fast. Some sounds with high pitch are a cat's meow and a child's voice. The faster the vibrations, the higher the pitch. A whistle makes faster vibrations than a bullfrog's croak.

▼ **Which dog's bark has a higher pitch?**

 What kind of vibrations do you think a bird's chirp makes? Why?

Think, Talk, and Write

1. **Predict.** What will happen when a guitar string stops vibrating?

2. What is pitch?

3. Write about a sound you heard today. Describe its pitch and volume.

Music Link

Which instrument has a low pitch? Which instrument has a high pitch? What do they look like?

Sound Off!

Think about the sounds you hear every day. Some sounds are loud, and others are soft. Some sounds are high, and others are low.

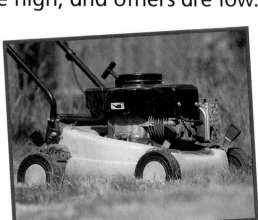

 Write About It

Describe the pitch and volume of a sound you hear every day. How do we use sounds? Why are sounds important?

Remember

When you describe something, you give details.

 e-Journal Write about it online @ **www.macmillanmh.com**

 ELA W 2.2.I. Write brief narratives based on their experiences.

Drum Fun

Miss Lee sells four different drums in her store. The first drum is 10 centimeters wide. The second drum is 20 centimeters wide. The third drum is 30 centimeters wide.

10 cm	20 cm	30 cm	?

Follow the Pattern

How wide is the fourth drum?
Follow this number pattern:

10 + 10 = 20

20 + 10 = 30

30 + ? = ?

Miss Lee knows that the smallest drum has the highest pitch. Which drum has the lowest pitch?

Remember
You can use a pattern to help you solve problems.

MA SDAP 2.2.0. Students demonstrate an understanding of patterns and how patterns grow and describe them in general ways.

Weight in Space

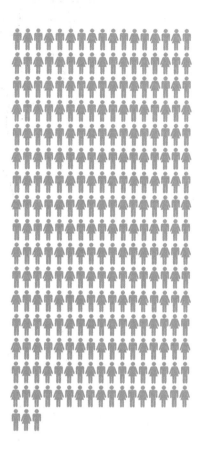

Gravity pulls things toward the center of Earth with a force. The amount of this force is called weight. How much do you weigh? Many students your age weigh about 60 pounds. How much does an elephant weigh? A male elephant can weigh 16,500 pounds! That is as much as 275 second graders!

strongest

All planets and moons have a force of gravity. Some planets and moons have more gravity than Earth. Other objects in space have less. The planet with the strongest force of gravity is Jupiter.

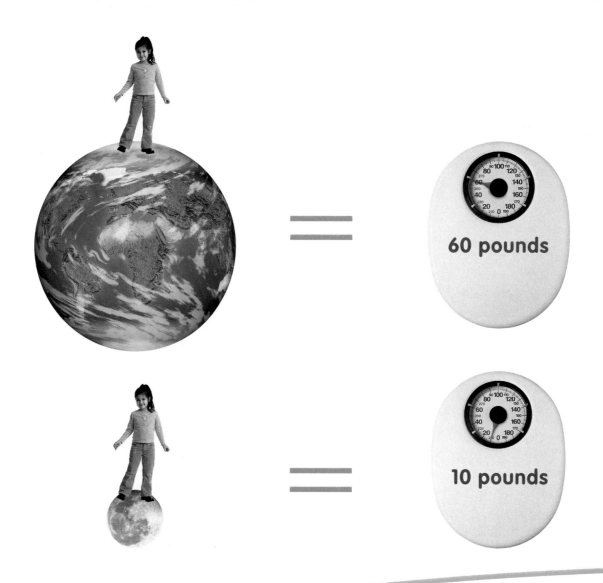

60 pounds

10 pounds

Our Moon has less gravity than Earth has. The Moon is smaller than Earth. There is less force that pulls things down. On the Moon, you would weigh less. You would weigh as much as a cat on Earth!

Since there is less gravity on the Moon, people can jump higher there. Astronauts bounced high when they walked on the Moon. If you threw a ball on the Moon, it would fly very far. In a baseball game, you would hit a homerun every time! What could you do if there was less gravity pulling you down?

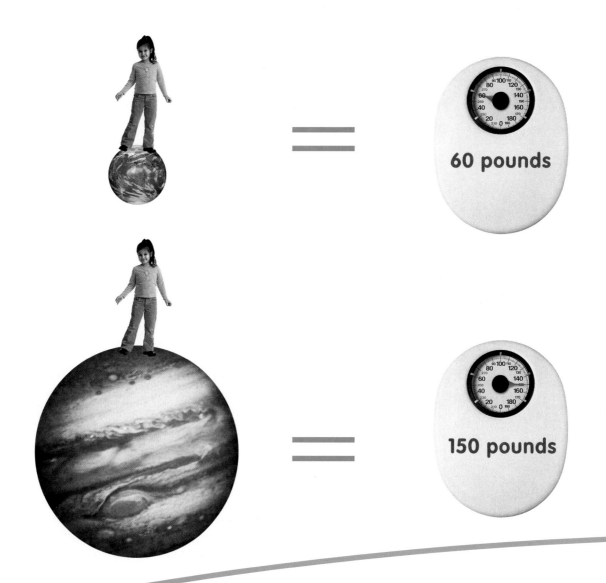

60 pounds

150 pounds

Some planets are much bigger than Earth. Objects weigh more on these bigger planets. There is more force that pulls things down. On Jupiter, you would weigh about twice as much as you weigh on Earth. Your arms would weigh twice as much! How would it feel to throw a baseball?

Some things might be easier to do on Jupiter. Imagine how fast you could skate down a hill. There would be more gravity pulling you down! What else could be good about the gravity on Jupiter?

Vocabulary

pitch, page 336	**ramp**, page 309	**weight**, page 318
poles, page 326	**volume**, page 334	

Use each word once for items 1-5.

1. Gravity pulls things toward the center of Earth with a certain amount of force. This amount of force is called _____. 2 PS 1.e

2. The loudness of a sound is called its _____. 2 PS 1.g

3. A _____ can make moving an object easier. 2 PS 1.d

4. Sounds can be high, low, or in between. This is called its _____. 2 PS 1.g

5. This magnet has two _____. 2 PS 1.f

6. How do wheels help people do work? 2 PS I.d

7. Describe how gravity affects the children on this sled. Why do you think it is harder to climb up a hill than to go down a hill? 2 PS I.e

8. Describe some ways we use magnets in the kitchen. 2 PS I.f

 What can forces do? 2 PS I.d

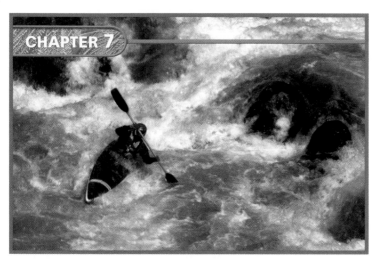

CHAPTER 7

Magnet Maze

▶ Draw a maze on a piece of paper. Put a magnet under the paper to move a paper clip through the maze. Have a partner time how long it takes to finish the maze.

▶ Move the magnet away from the paper and try the maze again. Why do you think it took longer to finish the maze?

▶ What would happen if you used a plastic checker instead of a paper clip? Why?

▶ What other objects could you use in your magnet maze?

348

2 PS I.f. Students know magnets can be used to make some objects move without being touched.

1 **What would happen if you threw a ball and there were no gravity?** 2 PS I.e

   A It would fall back toward the ground.

   B It would fly off into the air and not come down.

   C It would be attracted to a magnet.

   D It would make a sound.

2 **The picture below shows a hammer.**

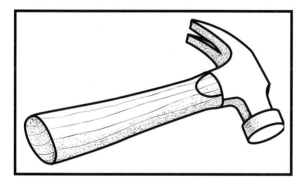

   What does this tool do? 2 PS I.d

   A makes work easier

   B makes pitch higher

   C grows plants

   D attracts iron

3 **What would a magnet attract?** 2 PS I.f

   A a penny

   B a piece of paper

   C a paper clip

   D a marble

Echolocation

Sounds are all around you, but can sound vibrations help you get dinner? If you are a bat, the answer is yes! Bats use echolocation to move around and catch food.

Bats live in caves. They can not see very well in the dark. They use sound to help them fly and find food in the dark.

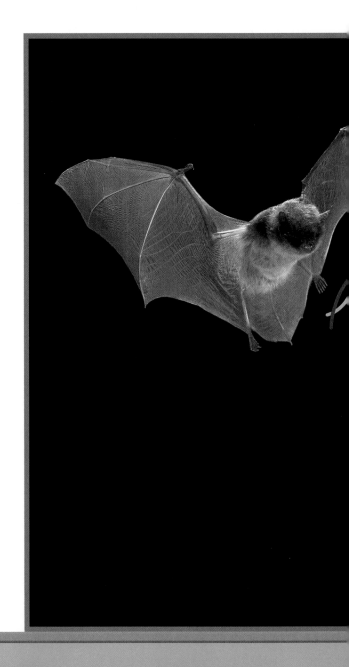

 2 PS I.g. Students know sound is made by vibrating objects and can be described by its pitch and volume.
ELA R 2.2.0. Students read and understand grade-level appropriate material.

First, the bat makes a high pitched squeak. The sound vibrations from the squeak move through the air and hit a moth. The vibrations bounce off the moth and come back to the bat. Then the bat swoops down and catches the moth for a meal.

▲ Bats are not the only animals that use echolocation. Dolphins make clicking noises to help find food.

◀ The bat uses sound to hunt for food.

Careers in Science

Crash Tester

If you like to learn about cars and safety, you could become a crash tester. Crash testers learn how to make cars safer by setting up crashes!

These workers explore what happens to dummies, or big dolls, in a car crash. Then the crash testers decide how to make the cars safer. Crash testers study different air bags and seat belts and find ways to make them safer.

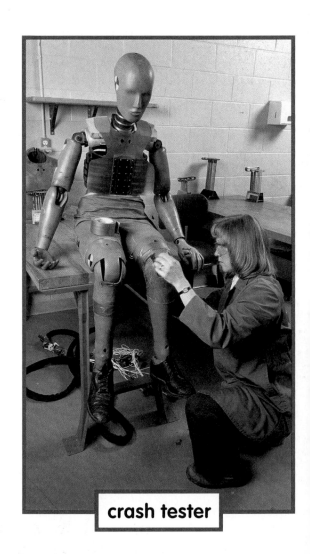

crash tester

More Careers to Think About

mechanic

car designer

LOG ON e-Careers @ www.macmillanmh.com

Reference

▶ You can use a balance to compare two objects.

Science Content Standards

Physical Sciences

I. **The motion of objects can be observed and measured. As a basis for understanding this concept:**

   a. *Students know* the position of an object can be described by locating it in relation to another object or to the background.

   b. *Students know* an object's motion can be described by recording the change in position of the object over time.

   c. *Students know* the way to change how something is moving is by giving it a push or a pull. The size of the change is related to the strength, or the amount of force, of the push or pull.

   d. *Students know* tools and machines are used to apply pushes and pulls (forces) to make things move.

   e. *Students know* objects fall to the ground unless something holds them up.

   f. *Students know* magnets can be used to make some objects move without being touched.

   g. *Students know* sound is made by vibrating objects and can be described by its pitch and volume.

Life Sciences

2. **Plants and animals have predictable life cycles. As a basis for understanding this concept:**

   a. *Students know* that organisms reproduce offspring of their own kind and that the offspring resemble their parents and one another.

   b. *Students know* the sequential stages of life cycles are different for different animals, such as butterflies, frogs, and mice.

   c. *Students know* many characteristics of an organism are inherited from the parents. Some characteristics are caused or influenced by the environment.

   d. *Students know* there is variation among individuals of one kind within a population.

   e. *Students know* light, gravity, touch, or environmental stress can affect the germination, growth, and development of plants.

   f. *Students know* flowers and fruits are associated with reproduction in plants.

Earth Sciences

3. **Earth is made of materials that have distinct properties and provide resources for human activities. As a basis for understanding this concept:**

   a. *Students know* how to compare the physical properties of different kinds of rocks and know that rock is composed of different combinations of minerals.

   b. *Students know* smaller rocks come from the breakage and weathering of larger rocks.

   c. *Students know* that soil is made partly from weathered rock and partly from organic materials and that soils differ in their color, texture, capacity to retain water, and ability to support the growth of many kinds of plants.

   d. *Students know* that fossils provide evidence about the plants and animals that lived long ago and that scientists learn about the past history of Earth by studying fossils.

   e. *Students know* rock, water, plants, and soil provide many resources, including food, fuel, and building materials, that humans use.

Investigation and Experimentation

4. **Scientific progress is made by asking meaningful questions and conducting careful investigations. As a basis for understanding this concept and addressing the content in the other three strands, students should develop their own questions and perform investigations. Students will:**

   a. Make predictions based on observed patterns and not random guessing.

   b. Measure length, weight, temperature, and liquid volume with appropriate tools and express those measurements in standard metric system units.

   c. Compare and sort common objects according to two or more physical attributes (e.g., color, shape, texture, size, weight).

   d. Write or draw descriptions of a sequence of steps, events, and observations.

   e. Construct bar graphs to record data, using appropriately labeled axes.

   f. Use magnifiers or microscopes to observe and draw descriptions of small objects or small features of objects.

   g. Follow oral instructions for a scientific investigation.

Recycle

It is important to recycle so we have clean air, water, and land.

▲ To help take care of Earth, recycle as much as you can.

▲ When you see this symbol on something, you can recycle the object.

▲ You can use things more than one time.

Clean Up

We need to keep workplaces clean.
Put things where they belong.

▲ It is important to wash your hands.

▲ If something breaks, do not touch it. Let an adult clean up the broken pieces.

◄ Wear a smock or apron so you do not get paint on your clothes.

357

Care of Plants

Taking care of plants helps you learn about their needs.

▲ Put plants in a sunny place.

▶ Give plants plenty of water.

Care of Animals

Taking care of animals helps you learn about their needs.

▶ Give animals a safe place to live.

▶ Be kind to pets. Handle them with care.

▶ Give pets food and water.

▶ Do not touch wild animals. They might bite, sting, or scratch you.

▶ Do not touch things in places where wild animals live.

359

Use a Bar Graph

You can use a bar graph to organize data. The title of the graph tells you the topic of what you are recording. The shaded bars tell you how much of each thing there is.

What was the class's favorite fruit?

Favorite Fruits

Try It

Make your own bar graph to show your class's favorite fruits.

How to Measure

You can use objects to measure. Line up the objects and count them. Use objects that are alike. They must be the same size.

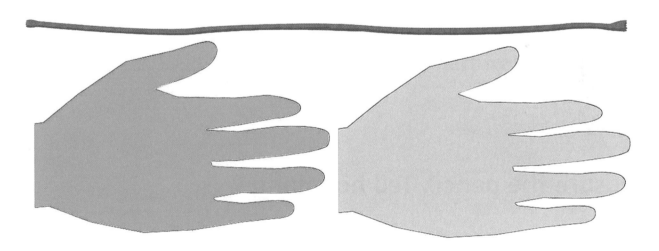

▲ This string is about 8 paper clips long.

▲ This string is about 2 hands long.

Try It

Measure some string. Tell how you did it.

Measure in Centimeters

You can use a ruler to measure solids. You can use centimeters (cm). This is called a unit of measurement.

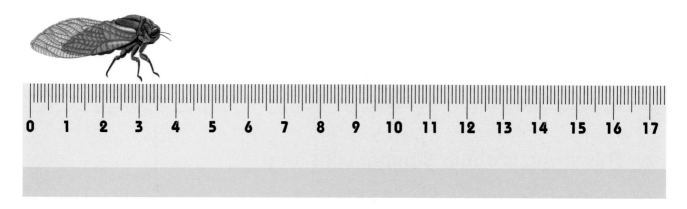

▲ You can measure this fly in centimeters. Line up the end of the fly with the 0 on the ruler. The fly is about 4 centimeters long. This is written as 4 cm.

Try It

Measure the pencil. Tell how long it is.

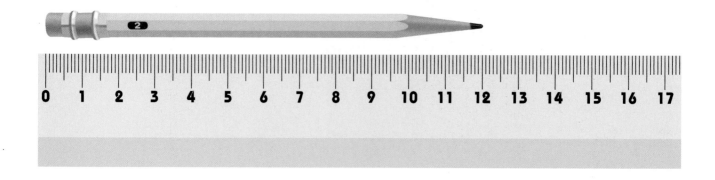

Measure in Inches

You can use inches (in.) to measure, too.
This toy is 3 inches, or 3 in., long.

Inches

You can predict how long something is.
When you predict, you guess the length.
Then you can use a ruler to measure it.

Try It

Predict how long
each object is.
Then use a ruler to
measure the objects.

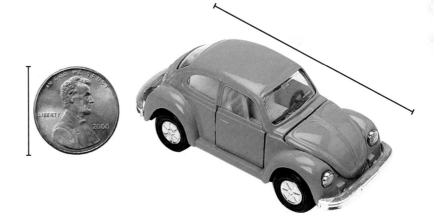

Object	Predict	Measure
penny	about ___ in.	___ in.
toy car	about ___ in.	___ in.

You can use a measuring cup to measure liquids. A measuring cup measures volume. Volume is the amount of space a liquid takes up. Liquids can take up different amounts of space.

Try It

1. Find a container. Predict how much orange juice it can hold.

2. Fill the container with orange juice. Measure the juice in cups. Was your prediction right?

Use a Balance

A balance measures mass. It lets you compare the mass of two different objects.

Place one object on each side of the balance. The object that has more mass will make that side of the balance go down. The object with less mass will go up.

Try It

Place two objects on a balance. Which has more mass?

Before you compare masses, make sure the arrow points to the line.

Use a Scale

A scale measures weight. You can measure weight in pounds (lbs). You can measure the weight of fruits and vegetables. You can measure your weight, too.

Try It

1. What is your weight? First predict your weight. Then use a scale to measure it.

2. Every month, measure your weight. Record it in a chart. See how your weight changes as you grow.

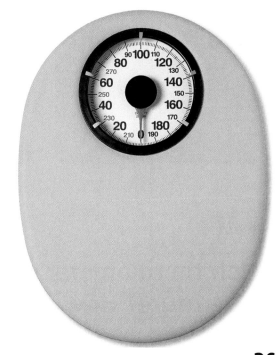

Use a Thermometer

A thermometer measures temperature. There is liquid inside the thermometer. When it gets warmer, the liquid moves up. When it gets cooler, the liquid moves down.

Try It

Which thermometer shows a warmer temperature? How can you tell?

A thermometer has marks with numbers. The marks show degrees Fahrenheit and degrees Celsius.

Read this thermometer in degrees Fahrenheit. Look at the numbers on the left side. Find the number where the liquid ends.

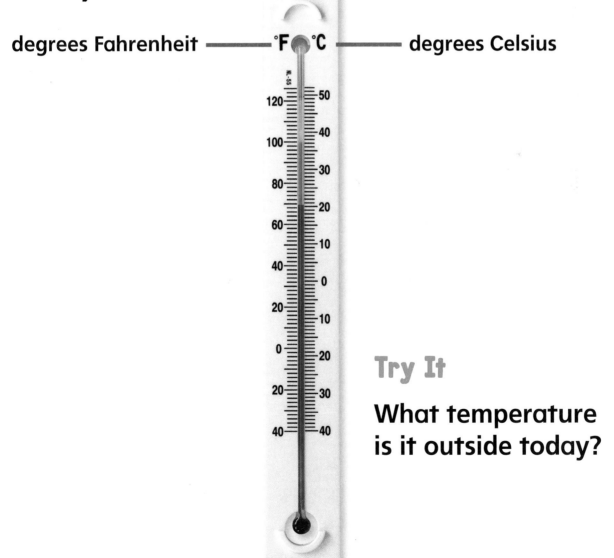

degrees Fahrenheit — °F °C — degrees Celsius

Try It

What temperature is it outside today?

Use Weather Tools

You can use weather tools to measure the weather.

▶ **A thermometer tells you how hot or cool the air is.**

▲ A rain gauge tells you how much rain falls. It has a ruler to measure the amount of rain in the jar.

Some weather tools help measure wind.

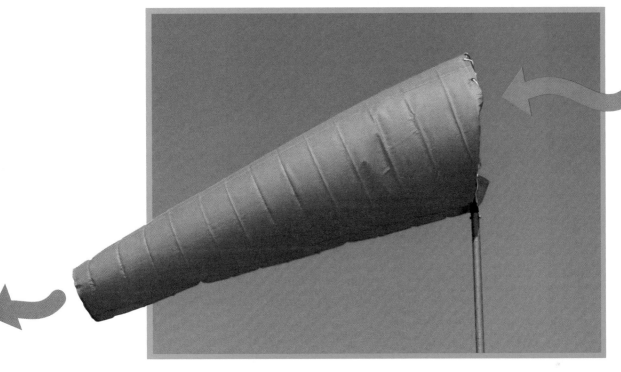

▲ A wind vane tells which way the wind blows.

▶ An anemometer measures how fast the wind blows. It tells the speed of the wind.

Try It

Use a rain gauge. Measure how much rain falls on two rainy days.

A clock measures time.

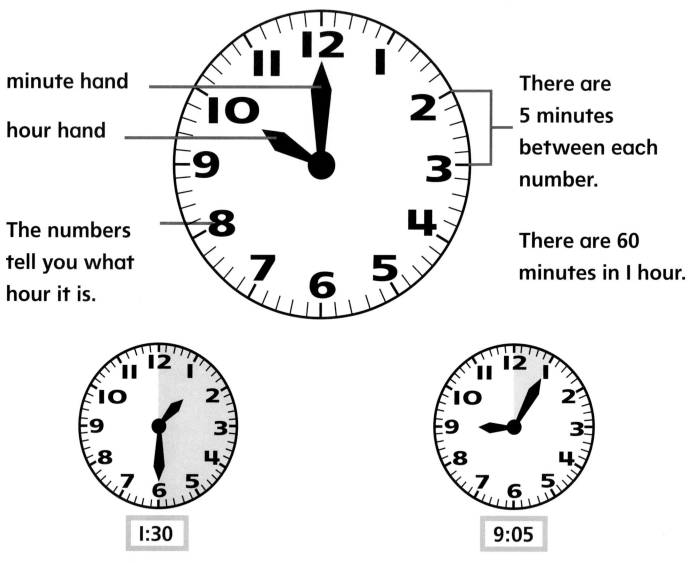

minute hand

hour hand

The numbers tell you what hour it is.

There are 5 minutes between each number.

There are 60 minutes in 1 hour.

| 1:30 |
30 minutes after 1 o'clock

| 9:05 |
5 minutes after 9 o'clock

Try It

Predict how long you sleep each night. Then use a clock to find out.

Use a Hand Lens

A hand lens makes objects seem larger. Scientists use them to get a closer look at objects.

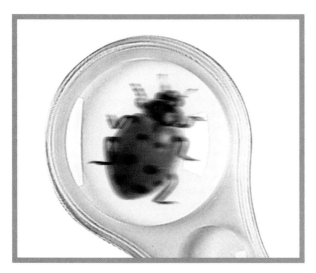

First, move the lens away from the object. Stop when the object looks fuzzy.

Next, move the lens a little closer to the object. Stop when the object looks clear.

Try It

1. Observe each bug here. Use a hand lens.

2. How many legs do you see on the bugs?

3. What else can you see?

Use a Computer

You can use a computer to get information. The Internet is a way to get a lot of information. It links your computer to other computers far away.

▲ When using a computer, make sure an adult knows what you are working on.

Try It

Use the Internet. Learn more about science in your world @ www.macmillanmh.com

Glossary

amphibians Amphibians are animals that live on both land and water. (page 78)

attract When a magnet attracts a metal, the magnet pulls the metal. (page 324)

classify Classify means to group things that are alike. (page 81)

communicate Communicate means to write, draw, or tell others your ideas. (page 82)

compare Compare means you tell how things are alike and different. (page 138)

distance Distance is how far away one thing is from another. (page 264)

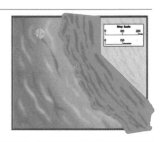

draw conclusions Draw conclusions means to use what you observe to explain what happens. (page 159)

extinct When a living thing is extinct, it has died out. None of its kind lives on Earth. (page 188)

flower A flower is the part of a plant that makes seeds. (page 30)

force Force is a push or pull used to put something in motion. (page 278)

fossil A fossil is what is left of a living thing from the past. (page 176)

friction Friction is a force that slows down moving things. (page 286)

fruit A fruit is the part of a plant that keeps seeds safe. (page 31)

fuel Fuel is something that gives off heat when it burns. (page 229)

G

geologist A geologist is a scientist who studies rocks and puts them into groups. (page 132)

germinate When a seed germinates, it begins to grow. (page 55)

gravity Gravity is a force that pulls things toward Earth. (page 316)

H

hardness When you describe a rock's hardness, you describe how tough it is. (page 137)

I

infer When you infer, you use what you know to figure something out. (page 175)

L

larva A larva is a young animal that hatches from an egg. The larva looks very different from the adult animal. (page 96)

lever A lever is a simple machine that lets you use less force to lift something. (page 308)

life cycle A life cycle is a group of steps that show how a living thing grows, changes, and makes new living things. (page 48)

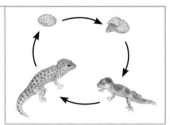

luster Luster is how a mineral looks when a light shines on it. (page 136)

 M

mammals Mammals are animals that have hair or fur. They feed their young milk. (page 78)

measure When you measure, you find out how long, how much, or how warm something is. (page 266)

minerals Minerals make up rocks. Some rocks are made of many minerals. (page 143)

molting Molting happens when an animal comes out of its hard shell to grow bigger. (page 97)

motion Motion is a change in position. (page 271)

 N

natural resource A natural resource is something from Earth that people use. (page 216)

 O

observe Observe means to find out information. When you observe something, you carefully look, hear, taste, touch, or smell it. (page 32)

paleontologist A paleontologist is a scientist who studies fossils. (page 186)

pistil A pistil is the part of a flower that takes in pollen and makes seeds. (page 36)

pistil

pitch Pitch describes how high or low a sound is. (page 336)

poles Magnets have two poles. The poles are where the pull of the magnet is strongest. (page 326)

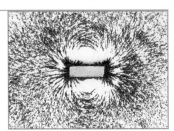

pollen Pollen is a sticky powder inside flowers. It helps make seeds. (page 36)

population A population is a group of the same kind of plants or animals. They share many traits. (page 106)

position Position is the place where something is. (page 262)

predict Predict means to use what you know to tell what will happen. (page 312)

property A property tells you something about an object. (page 136)

pull When you pull something, you move it closer to you. (page 279)

pupa A pupa is made when a larva forms a hard case around its body. Inside the case, the larva grows into an adult. (page 99)

push When you push something, you move it away from you. (page 279)

R

ramp A ramp is a simple machine that helps you move things to a higher place. (page 309)

record data When you record data, you write down what you observe. (page 329)

repel When two poles of magnets repel, they push away from each other. (page 327)

reptiles Reptiles are animals that have scales and are cold-blooded. Most reptiles lay eggs. (page 78)

S

seed coat A seed coat is a cover that keeps a seed safe and keeps it from drying out. (page 39)

seeds Seeds are made by flowers. They can grow into new plants. (page 31)

sequence A sequence tells the order in which things happen. When you describe a sequence, you tell which comes first, next, and last. (page 180)

simple machine A simple machine can make the force of your push or pull stronger. (page 308)

skeleton A skeleton is an animal's full set of bones. (page 189)

soil Soil is made up of rocks and tiny bits of dead plants and animals. (page 152)

solar power Things that run on solar power use sunlight to make electric power. (page 236)

sound Sound is a kind of energy you hear. (page 332)

speed Speed is how far something moves in a certain amount of time. (page 272)

stamen The stamen is the part of a flower that makes pollen. (page 36)

stamen

 T

tool A tool is an object that helps you do work. (page 310)

trait A trait is a way plants and animals look like their parents. (page 47)

V

vibrates When something vibrates, it moves back and forth in a fast way. (page 332)

volume Volume describes the loudness of a sound. (page 334)

Credits

Photo Researchers, Inc. 178-179: Francois Gohier/Photo Researchers, Inc. 180: (tr)Holt Studios International Ltd/Alamy; (cl)Papilio/Alamy; (cr)Royalty-Free/CORBIS; (inset)Papilio/Alamy. 184-185: Jonathan Blair/CORBIS. 185: Jonathan Blair/CORBIS. 186: (l)Ken Lucas/Visuals Unlimited; (r)James L. Amos/National Geographic. 187: (tr)Peter Arnold, Inc./Alamy; (bl)Ken Lucas/Visuals Unlimited; (inset)Philip Lewis/Alamy. 188: Francis Latreille/CORBIS. 189: Francis Latreille/CORBIS. 191: Kjell B. Sandved/Visuals Unlimited. 192-193: D. Schwimmer/Bruce Coleman. 193: Juniors Bildarchiv/Alamy. 194: SOQUI TED/CORBIS SYGMA. 194-195: Philip James Corwin/CORBIS. 196: Francois Gohier/Photo Researchers, Inc. 196-197: Kevin Schafer/NHPA. 197: B.A.E. Inc./Alamy. 198: Photo by Dennis Finnin. Copyright American Museum of Natural History. 199: Copyright American Museum of Natural History. 200-201: James L. Amos/CORBIS. 202: (cr)Danita Delimont/Alamy; (b)John Cancalosi/AGEfotostock. 203: (cl)Layne Kennedy/CORBIS; (b)James L. Amos/CORBIS. 206: Lynton Gardiner/Dorling Kindersley, The American Museum of Natural History. 208: (tr)David Muench/CORBIS; (tc)David Muench/CORBIS; (l)Jeff Foott/Discovery Channel Images/PictureQuest; (c)Jeff Vanuga/naturepl.com. 214-215: Diana Koenigsberg/Botanica/Getty Images. 216: Mark A. Johnson/CORBIS. 217: (c)PhotoLink/Getty Images; (bl)Michael S. Yamashita/CORBIS; (bc)Juliette Wade/Dorling Kindersley; (br)Lester V. Bergman/CORBIS. 218: Andy Sacks/Getty Images. 218-219: Timothy O'Keefe/Bruce Coleman. 219: (tr) davies & starr/Getty Images; (cr)Demetrio Carrasco/Dorling Kindersley, Courtesy of the Hubbell Trading Post National Historic Site, Arizona. 220: (b)Bettmann/CORBIS; (inset)Lester Lefkowitz/CORBIS. 221: ML Sinibaldi/CORBIS. 223: PhotoLink/Getty Images. 224-225: Peter Adams/zefa/CORBIS. 226: (l)John Elk III/Lonely Planet Images/Getty Images; (inset)Brand X Pictures/PunchStock; (r)C Squared Studios/Getty Images; (bl)D. Hurst/Alamy; (br)RDF/Visuals Unlimited. 227: (bl)Photodisc/PunchStock; (bc)Gary Crabbe/Alamy; (br) Becky Luigart-Stayner/CORBIS. 228: (tr)Comstock Images/Alamy; (l)Royalty-Free/CORBIS; (c)Ingram Publishing/Alamy; (cr)Photodisc Collection/Getty Images; (br)Bruton-Stroube Studios/FoodPix/PictureQuest. 229: allOver photography/Alamy. 231: (bl)G.K. & Vikki Hart/Getty Images; (bc)G.K. & Vikki Hart/Getty Images; (br) Jules Frazier/Photodisc/Getty Images. 232-233: Julie Houck/CORBIS. 233: (tl)Worldwide Picture Library/Alamy; (tr)Jeremy Horner/CORBIS. 234-235: Kyle Newton/Getty Images. 236: Lester Lefkowitz/Getty Images. 237: (tr)Thinkstock/Alamy; (b)G. Brad Lewis/Photo Researchers, Inc.; (inset)Brand X Pictures/Alamy. 238: (b)Craig Lovell/CORBIS; (inset)Mark Thomas/FoodPix/PictureQuest. 239: Getty Images; (inset)Royalty-Free/CORBIS. 240: (c)imagebroker/Alamy; (inset)Inga Spence/Visuals Unlimited. 241: (tr)Hulton Archive/Getty Images; (l)Eric Nathan/Alamy. 242-243: AGStockUSA, Inc./Alamy. 244: Peter Arnold, Inc./Alamy. 245: Roger Ball/CORBIS. 246: (c)Royalty-Free/CORBIS; (r)Amy Etra/Photo Edit. 246-247: Fernando Bueno/Getty Images. 248: (cl)Brand X Pictures/Alamy; (bl)G. Brad Lewis/Photo Researchers, Inc. 250: DAVE BARTRUFF/DanitaDelimont.com. 262: (l)Ken Lucas/Getty Images; (r)Jane Burton/Dorling Kindersley/Getty Images. 265: (l)Chris Mattison/Dorling Kindersley; (c)Kim Taylor/Dorling Kindersley; (r)Amos Morgan/Getty Images. 268-269: Lester Lefkowitz/CORBIS. 270: (l)Photodisc/Getty Images; (r)Photodisc/Getty Images. 271: Photodisc/Getty Images. 272: Mark Scott/Getty Images. 273: (t to b)Photodisc/Getty Images; Geoff Dann/Dorling Kindersley; Digital Vision/PunchStock. 276-27: Mike Brinson/Getty Images. 278: (r)Photodisc/Getty Images; (bl)Rubberball/PictureQuest. 279: (c)Norbert Schaefer/CORBIS; (b)Rolf Bruderer/CORBIS. 280: Jeff Greenberg/Photo Edit. 282: (bl, br)NRM/SSPL/The Image Works. 283: (tl)Underwood & Underwood/CORBIS; (r)Robert Mullan/Alamy; (b)Carphotos/Alamy. 284-285: Michael Wong/Getty Images. 286: (l to r) f1 online/Alamy; K-PHOTOS/Alamy; David Young-Wolff/Photo Edit; Richard Hutchings/Photo Edit. 287: (r)Ron Chapple/Getty Images; (b)Royalty-Free/CORBIS. 288: (r)Robert W. Ginn/Photo Edit; (bl)Peter Arnold, Inc./Alamy. 289: Scott T. Baxter/Getty Images. 290: Doug Allen/naturepl.com. 298: (cr)Comstock Images/Alamy; (br)Seiya Kawamoto/Getty Images. 299: Photodisc/Getty Images. 300: (tl)Purestock/Alamy; (tr)Balfour Studios/Alamy; (c)Michael Newman/Photo Edit. 306-307: David Young-Wolff/Photo Edit. 309: (tr)Steve Cole/Photodisc Red/Getty Images; (b)Spencer Grant/Photo Edit. 310-311: Thinkstock/Getty Images. 311: (t)foodfolio/Alamy; (r)Kevin Summers/Getty Images. 314-315: H. Spichtinger/zefa/Corbis. 315: (t to b)Royalty-free/Corbis; Royalty-free/CORBIS; Felicia Martinez/Photo Edit. 316: Kevin R. Morris/CORBIS. 318: (l)Maximilian Weinzierl/Alamy; (r)PhotoLink/Getty Images. 319: Digital image © 1996 CORBIS; Original image courtesy of NASA/CORBIS. 320: (tr)Photo by Denis Finnin. Copyright American Museum of Natural History; (bl)Jean-Charles Cuillandre/CFHT/Photo Researchers, Inc. 320-321: Roger Ressmeyer/CORBIS. 324: Photolibrary.com Pty. Ltd./Index Stock Imagery. 325: Tim Ridley/Dorling Kindersley. 326: (tr)Planetary Visions Ltd / Photo Researchers, Inc.; (b)Photolibrary.com Pty. Ltd./IndexStock. 338: (tl)Robert Slade/Alamy; (tr)Gary W. Carter/CORBIS; (cl)Robert W. Ginn/Photo Edit; (cr)Craig Orsini/Index Stock Imagery. 340: Art Wolfe/Getty Images. 341: William Radcliffe/Science Faction/Getty Images. 343: Digital Vision/Getty Images. 344: Don Farrall/Photodisc Green/Getty Images. 345: (t)Antonio M Rosario/Getty Images; (inset)Royalty-Free/CORBIS; (bkgd)B & M Productions. 347: Jeff Cadge/Getty Images.

Acknowledgments: "Dinosaur Bone" from *Keepers* by Alice Schertle. Copyright © 1996 by Alice Schertle. Used by permission of Lothrop, Lee, and Shepard Books, a division of William Morrow & Co., Inc.

"If" from *Popcorn Poems* by James Stevenson. Copyright © 1998 by James Stevenson. Published by Greenwillow Books, a division of William Morrow & Co. All rights reserved.

"In Payment" and "Under a Stone" from *Out in the Dark and Daylight* by Aileen Fisher. Copyright © 1980 by Aileen Fisher. Published by Harper & Row Publishers. All rights reserved.

"Sun" and "Magnet" from *all the small poems and fourteen more* by Valerie Worth. Poems copyright © 1994 by Valerie Worth. Published by Farrar, Straus & Giroux. All rights reserved.

"The Seed" from *Always Wondering* by Aileen Fisher. Copyright © 1991 by Aileen Fisher. HarperCollins Publishers. Used by permission of the author, who controls all rights.